ENDORSEM

It is very rare to find a book written on the authenticity of angelic presence. The very existence of the angelic ministry is given as a strategy and a promise from the Father Almighty to every believer. Every candidate who is an heir of salvation is also given not only eternal life, but also an eternal assistant, an eternal adjutant, confidant, and a detailed concierge that does more than watch over us while we sleep. Angels support us in all of our ways, lest we dash our feet against the rocks of life.

Lenika Scott goes far beyond literary accuracy, she has categorized the function of angels, the protection of angels, the ministry of angels, and how to dispatch angels and assign them. She has methodically, with precise specificity, opened the eyes of every reader to her encounters with angels. It's not a spooky book nor a fairy-tale composition. This is a handbook on how to benefit from a most precious asset given to every believer in the household of faith. You will see and recall many times in your life when things happened that were unexplainable.

This book awakens your sensitivity to angels. You will learn how to dispatch them by your words. Many people live out their entire journey as a Kingdom citizen yet never use their supernatural adjutant. Wouldn't it be a shame to get to Heaven and see all of the angels given to you to assist you and regret how much you struggled when you could have taken advantage of an angelic presence that was granted to you at the very gate of salvation. Father God gave them to us for a reason. The true fact is they are given by the Father and they are given a specific duty to assist the believer.

This is indeed a must-read book. I can promise you it will be a book that you can't put down once you start a journey into the pages. For every chapter that you engage, you will be given the opportunity to be a doer and not just a casual observer. You need supernatural assistance in this complex life that we are facing today. Why deny yourself the divine help given to you by your Creator who knows all things. Jesus Himself had angels at His command. He actually said that He could call a legion of them and they would harken to His word. It's time for you to put your angels to work. It's time to give them assignments of assistance. They are your supernatural personal assistants. They are waiting for your words. They are ready to carry you through the storms and adversities of life.

I would never venture to journey into some of the dangerous and hostile territories that I navigate if it were not for the divine protection of my angels. I command them to hold up every plane I'm on when the flight is experiencing intense turbulence. You can command them to protect your children, your properties, your business, and so much more. Many times we are entertaining angels unaware, so be careful how you treat the people you interact with.

This is an invitation to come and learn about the ministry of angels from a very sober and grave author who has taken the responsibility to back up every claim with the Word of God, which is the very highest authority. Get ready for your life to be transformed. Get ready to end the struggles of your life. Get ready to release your angelic agents on an assignment and watch the supernatural outcome. This book will change your life and your perspective of life forever. It's now time to read and become a serious student and recipient of the ministry of angels.

Dr. Patricia Bailey
Founder of Master's Touch Ministries Global Inc. Outreach Ministry
Winston-Salem, North Carolina

I've always known Lenika to a have a very strong hunger for the things of God. She's always wanted more of Him. Her heart for His people has always been huge and she has a very strong spirit of discernment. My perspective is that prayer is paramount to success, and I've personally seen God work emotional, physical, and financial miracles in her life due to her life of intercession. If you are ready to break barriers and go much further, *Angelic Allies* is the perfect book to read and grow in God and develop a deeper understanding of the supernatural.

Dr. Jewel Tankard
Co-Pastor of Destiny Center
Murfreesboro, Tennessee

Lenika Scott, has revealed to the world through this mission, *Angelic Allies*, the times and seasons we are in with divine angelic activities. I believe she carries an Issachar spirit, the ability to discern the times and seasons we are in with angels. God has given her great revelation concerning angels through many supernatural encounters with them. Because of her persistent prayer life and her hunger and thirst for the deep things of God, He has chosen her to be a trailblazer to release great depth of understanding about angels and share supernatural encounters with them.

God has chosen her prophetic voice to be a mouthpiece for Him in these last days. Lenika's wisdom and desire to see the body of Christ exposed to the *greater* has been released in detail in this book. I have known Lenika for many years and once pastored her and her family. Since knowing her, she has always pursued for the more and deep things of the Spirit. She has the anointing, wisdom, and revelation to write such an amazing book that challenges all of us to believe God for more than a Sunday Service. This book will elevate you and cause you to become hungry and thirsty for the deep things of God again. If you are ready to go deeper in the Spirit, this book is for you.

Apostle Matthew Tillery
Pastor of Tri-Faith Ministries
Rocky Mount, North Carolina

Angelic Allies was written with much passion, insight, experience, love, grace, and wisdom. God always prepares the believer for what He's about to unfold in their lives. I recall a very prophetic conversation that Lenika and I shared. She spoke what God was descending from Heaven as a download. She declared that God was giving her an angel book, and she immediately began to seek Him for divine revelation that was to be penned for His purpose.

People of God, spiritual warfare is real and so many in the body of Christ do not know exactly how to engage or even know the access that they have for help! We have angelic hosts at our disposal that can be dispatched on our and others' behalf, but we need that knowledge. Well, God has called forth one of His angels here on earth to put the tool in our hands for us to be enlightened and also to dig deeper concerning the spiritual realm. Be encouraged, be inspired, and allow this book to elevate you into the realms of glory. Now, grow in His grace!

CO-PASTOR KIMBERLY CANTY
Living Waters Christian Ministries
Spartanburg, South Carolina

In *Angelic Allies,* Lenika Scott stirs your heart to go deeper into the supernatural treasures of God. Though this book is about the angelic, the personal testimonies and truth will create a hunger in your soul for more intimacy with God the Father, the Son, and the Holy Spirit. This book will literally woo you into the hidden things of God. I have witnessed Lenika's unwavering walk with the Lord for twenty years, and I rejoice in all that He is doing through her today! Everything she describes in these pages is for *you* as well. Glean from her maturity and wisdom as you read this book. You too can have great intimacy with the Father, which produces the supernatural angelic activity in your life. God is the same yesterday, today, and forever.

BETH K. FERRELL
Intercessor
Apex, North Carolina

ANGELIC ALLIES

ANGELIC ALLIES

GOD'S MESSENGERS, GOD'S WARRIORS, GOD'S AGENTS

LENIKA SCOTT

DESTINY IMAGE® PUBLISHERS, INC.

P.O. Box 310, Shippensburg, PA 17257-0310

"Promoting Inspired Lives."

This book and all other Destiny Image and Destiny Image Fiction books are available at Christian bookstores and distributors worldwide.

Cover design by Eileen Rockwell
Interior design by Terry Clifton

For more information on foreign distributors, call 717-532-3040.

Reach us on the Internet: www.destinyimage.com.

ISBN 13 TP: 978-0-7684-5102-3
ISBN 13 eBook: 978-0-7684-5103-0
ISBN 13 HC: 978-0-7684-5105-4
ISBN 13 LP: 978-0-7684-5104-7

For Worldwide Distribution, Printed in the U.S.A.
1 2 3 4 5 6 7 8 / 23 22 21 20 19

DEDICATION

This book is dedicated to the Holy Trinity—God the Father, Jesus, and precious Holy Spirit.

God, You have taught me a Father's love, corrected me when I needed it, and elevated me to places unimaginable. You've really opened this Scripture to me, *"That thine alms may be in secret: and thy Father which seeth in secret himself shall reward thee openly"* (Matthew 6:4 KJV). To my precious *Jesus,* though I've yet to see You face to face, I will never forget when You showed up behind me while I was ministering. Such holiness permeated around Your being. *Holy Spirit,* You have taught me so much and I am so thankful and grateful You arrested me at a young age. You've taught me how to surrender my life and my heart to Holy God. You've taught me how to pray, how to preserve and stand on the Word even under uncertainty and resistance. I can go on and on…but I want to thank You for the lifelong journey to come. I am blessed, thankful, and grateful.

Acknowledgments

I acknowledge and thank my loving husband, Gregg Scott. You are my rock, my protector, and have been such a huge supporter during this writing process. To my six beautiful daughters—Jazmine, Janaé, Jayla, Joy, Jireh, Jordan, and granddaughter Anaya—thank you for your loving spirits, your kindnesses, and your patience as Mommy surrendered to the will of God.

CONTENTS

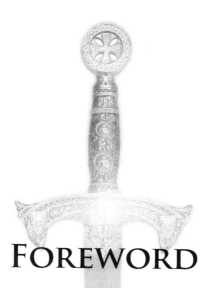

FOREWORD

Get ready for an adventure, a journey into the world of the supernatural and supernatural beings. You will be exposed to, introduced to, and educated about angels—God's supernatural agents. This book will create an appetite inside you for the supernatural. It is the who, what, when, where, why, and how of angels. This world is not a fairy-tale or a dream. This book is scripturally sound. As you go through the Scriptures, you will realize the relevance of angels. You will become even more aware of how often angels were present and their assignments.

As I began to read through the first few chapters, my heart began to race with a longing for the presence of God. I felt God's glory! I became even more aware of angels and their assignments and how they are to be part of my life. Angels are ministering spirits sent forth for me, an heir of salvation. What are my angels doing? Are they unemployed because of me? No longer! I don't have to wait for angels to appear; they are all around me. There are times when the presence of them is so strong that I know they're with me; and then there are those moments when I don't recognize them at all, but I know they're here!

I have known of Lenika Scott for several years, but over the past year we have become even more acquainted. My husband, William Porter, and I have the pleasure of being Lenika and her family's pastors. Lenika is a licensed and ordained minister of the gospel of Jesus Christ. She is a ministry gift and is called and operates as a prophet. I know she has experienced the presence of angels; and in obedience to the Holy Spirit, she has spent countless hours studying the Scriptures regarding them so that this book is anchored by the Word of God.

This book will create encounters with the manifested presence of God and the hosts of Heaven! As you read *Angelic Allies,* be prepared for an encounter with Almighty God and His angels!

DONNA PORTER, PASTOR
Household of Faith Ministries
Raleigh, North Carolina

PREFACE

I believe when we get to Heaven a screen will be shown to us of the times our guardian angels were there to help, assist, and protect us. We are going to be so amazed by all of the angelic and divine moments we experienced that we knew not of.

From Genesis to Revelation, there are many accounts of angels with such details in the Word of God. If angels were not significant or important, God would not have created them. The word "angel" is mentioned in the Bible almost 300 times.

I've been hosting a prayer movement for years; in fact, during the releasing of this book I've embarked upon my ten-year marker—yes, a decade! After praying for countless individuals over the past ten years, it was recently that the Lord allowed me to start openly sharing my angelic experiences and encounters. Shocking to me, many of His people were not knowledgeable of this topic from a *biblical* perspective.

I believe we are living in the last days; and if we are going to be as effective as our heavenly Father desires us to be, we must be well-equipped with knowledge and understanding about His Kingdom. One of the main assists we receive, aside from the Holy Spirit, is the assistance we receive from His holy angels.

I also believe the Church has studied about demons and deliverance for far too long, causing the teaching of angels to become minimized. This is not to minimize revelation that comes from being knowledgeable in the area of deliverance as it all indeed is supernatural; however, we must be aware of the assistance of these holy and divine creatures and we must be open to their presence and existence because of the great mission they are assigned, as they help believers with the will of God being accomplished on earth.

We must be reminded that our earthly knowledge is limited. Even Scripture declares we know in part and prophesy in part (1 Corinthians 13:9). The heavenly realm—which is the realm where God, Jesus, the Holy Spirit and His heavenly host exist—is far more vast and far more detailed than words can explain. For we must understand much of this from a spiritual perspective.

The awareness of the ministry of angels has been part of my life for years; and now having looked back, I realize that the Holy Spirit was teaching and training me for such a time as this. To teach and train His people about a realm that exists beyond our span of control.

Angelic Allies is not only full of Scripture references and sound from a biblical perspective, but it also uncovers various personal testimony experiences by many people. This book was written that you may be able to gain hope from the Word of God concerning your situation, and anything you may be personally dealing with, to help execute heavenly help and assistance. There is teaching as well as revelation in this book.

Allow your faith to be increased as you press in to believe the impossible while gaining knowledge and revelation. It is my prayer that this book will offer much hope, inspiration, and encouragement.

Author's Note: All testimonies of angelic encounters shared in this book, unless otherwise noted, are written by the author. All personal testimonies shared are written by the actual person who witnessed the angelic encounter or supernatural experience and, with permission, the person's name is cited.

INTRODUCTION

MY FIRST SUPERNATURAL ENCOUNTER

In 1998, I had a supernatural encounter with the Holy Spirit that would forever change my life. I wholeheartedly believe something happens to us when we have a true encounter with God. It is not our job to pursue "the supernatural" over pursuing God, but I do believe as we set our hearts on tapping into the supernatural with a sense of purity, we will be able to embark upon many mysteries that are often missed by a vast number of believers.

The purpose of this introduction is to lay a brief foundation. This will outline my encounter with the Lord and also shed light on God opening my eyes into the realm of the spirit to see angels and become aware of their existence.

I was born prematurely! It seems like the enemy tried to take me out before I could even enter the world—apparently he knew something about me. You see, when you are a chosen vessel of the King, all sorts of things will come to stop you, and it may even be at the point of your arrival. BUT GOD! He kept and protected me in the womb and months thereafter. The hand of God was always on my life when I was growing up as a child, through my teens, and into my college years. Though I'd backslide along the way, there was always a deep fear and reverence of the Lord. I gave my life back to Christ in 1997 when I was in my 20s and that is when things seriously began to unfold.

A DIVINE ENCOUNTER

The divine encounter with the Lord that would change my life happened on a Thursday morning back in October 1998. I had planned to start my daily regimen of prayer that morning, but right after I woke up and before I could even get out of the bed, the *fire of God* fell on me!

I remember my hands being on fire—and I mean on *fire*. Though I didn't understand it, I knew that something holy was going on within me, and I knew the Holy Spirit had everything to do with it.

I prayed that morning, but it wasn't a long prayer. I asked God what was happening. Before I could get the question out of my mouth, He instantly dropped a Scripture into my spirit—He said, "Luke 9:2," which says, *"He sent them to preach the kingdom of God and to heal the sick."*

My hands seemed to burn all day long! That is how intense it was at the time.

Shortly after that, I started feeling a piercing in my hands. In the center of my palms, I felt a very strong piercing. I continued to seek after God through all that had been happening. Then the manifestations of the anointing started to change. At times, I would feel my hands burning or they would tingle or I would feel heat or they even would feel numb. So then I began to seek Him differently. I began to ask questions such as, "God, who am I? What have You called me to do? What is happening to me? Why are You allowing me to experience these manifestations? What is the reason for this?"

My dreams began to intensify. My hearing from the Lord was growing stronger and stronger. Then He started taking me to the books of the prophets. He started to speak to me about ministry. I was thinking,

God, are You serious? Yes, I was wondering if I was hearing from the Lord correctly. He started impressing upon me to read and study the lives of the major and minor prophets and how prophets functioned in the New Testament as well.

I remember waking up during the middle of the night to go to the bathroom and He would say, "Jeremiah." The next day as I would start reading different chapters in the book of Jeremiah, I would be afraid. I would start repenting because of the harsh judgments I read about. Then God said, "This is not for you, this is for My people."

During the time all of this was transpiring, God led me to Ezekiel, chapter 3 and started confirming my calling. I thought, *Me a prophet? For real?* One day my sister-in-love Dawn called me and said, "Lenika, has God revealed to you your calling?"

I paused because I did not want to say anything about what had been happening. I said, "Why do you ask?"

She said, "Well…while I was in prayer this morning, a vision of your face appeared before me and I heard the Lord say these words, 'A prophet among My people.' Then He led me to read Ezekiel chapter 3, where He told Ezekiel to eat the scroll." This was such confirmation to me.

After she told me what happened, I blurted out and poured out to her the experiences I had been having—and the fact that the Lord had just shown me that same Scripture as well. Around the same time, God was also dealing with her regarding the prophetic calling on her life, and we would often turn to one another for prayer and guidance from the Holy Spirit.

What a process it has been—whew! I will not go into many of those details, perhaps that is for another book; but if God has called you to the office of a prophet, know that it will be a long process. In addition, some things that happen to you only come from Him teaching you. For it is a process of being molded, bruised and crushed, separated, misunderstood, and yielding to the Lord like no other.

Nevertheless, while we are on the subject, the following are some things that are important for me to share. As you are reading, some of what I write may resonate with you; particularly if there is a ministry call to the office of a prophet, you will certainly relate.

- The Holy Spirit will train you! It is a position that is given to you by God and not people!

- You will appear to others as a peculiar person. They will see you as "different." That is not altogether in a bad way, but they may think there is something strange about you. Others will not be able to figure you out. You will have to go through major rejection and isolation.

- There is a sense of abandonment, as well. When God sees you getting "too close" to others to the point where you are depending on them and not Him, there will be a quick severing!

- Sometimes abrupt situations will occur in your life, but as you look back, it will be for your own protection. For example, He may suddenly move you from a place or position if He foresees that remaining there or in that place will cause defilement to occur.

- There will be a deeper sensitivity to the spirit world of angels and demons and Heaven and hell. For example, right before a person dies, many times God will show and reveal it to His prophets. God has shown me a few people who were going to transition before it happened. He has shown me people whom the enemy was trying to take out prematurely so that I could stand in the gap and pray.

- Often during moments of transition, prophets will receive words of wisdom and words of knowledge with specific details concerning a person.

- Not all prophets are the same. Their mantles are very different. Some will have visions on a regular basis, and some will dream more than others. To some, there will just be a knowing.

As I even share this portion, if you are called to the office of a prophet, you have to keep your heart right and clean before God. You cannot get caught up in your title! You have to know and understand that even you, yes you, can miss what God is telling you. You do not know everything, and pride can definitely cause you to quickly fall. I am reminded of Paul as I write this portion of the book. Because of the glorious experiences that Paul witnessed, God allowed something in Paul's life that would keep him humble:

> *And lest I should be exalted above measure through the abundance of the revelations, there was given to me a thorn in the flesh, the messenger of satan to buffet me, lest I should be exalted above measure* (2 Corinthians 12:7).

This is why, *if* you are a prophet or even an apostle, you cannot allow the spirit of pride or haughtiness to rise up within you and win. *Yes*, it will arise. You will know a lot of information to which others are not privy. In addition, with that, there is a greater level of responsibility. You have to keep your heart before the Lord on a *consistent* basis.

Word of Caution: If you are called to function in the office of a prophet, *you must keep a prayer life laced with reading the Word of God.* When, and if, prayer and reading the Bible become out of alignment, you can quickly open the door to a spirit of divination. Have you ever wondered why many of the prophets, whom God cleaned up and is now using for His glory, attest to the fact that before they were even aware of the prophetic calling over their lives they were drawn to the occult or to psychic people, desiring to have a greater awareness of the supernatural? I know I just went off in another direction, but prayerfully it helped someone understand a little bit more regarding the prophetic ministry.

Furthermore, God responds to our prayers, our cries, and our seeking. I was not concerned with worldly things; my focus, my thoughts, and desires were on heavenly things. On that day when I first heard Him, He said, "My daughter who has been seeking Me with all of her heart deserves a divine visitation, and so shall she be honored with one," and my life has never been the same!

> *As long as the earth remains, there will be planting and harvest...* (Genesis 8:22 NLT).

The hours of praying, focusing, purity, interceding, fasting, obedience, hunger after God, holiness, righteousness, sacrifice and studying caught up with me. Around 2001, I started to experience visions of angels. God would allow me to see angels as white beams of light. He allowed me to see them in front of doors, standing in the four corners of a room. They would stand in front of an entrance, but He would also allow me to feel when they were present. For example, I would walk through a door and there would be a deep knowing that an angel was present.

As you allow the spirit of the Lord to operate in and through you, He will give you a greater and deeper understanding of *all* things, even the things of the supernatural. It is my prayer that this book will greatly bless your life, taking you deeper into realms of the supernatural you may not have witnessed before—and if you have witnessed, that your hunger will even grow deeper. *The Holy Spirit will teach you!*

> *But the anointing which you have received from Him abides in you, and you do not need that anyone teach you; but as the same anointing teaches you concerning all things, and is true, and is not a lie, and just as it has taught you, you will abide in Him* (1 John 2:27).

CHAPTER 1

JESUS'S MINISTRY
AND ANGELS

JESUS APPEARED IN OUR SERVICE

The King of Kings visited us during a church service where my husband and I were asked to minister for a session, sharing our experience as marketplace ministers. Our story is titled "From Food Stamps to Millions." Our financial breakthrough came from a life of surrendering and yielding to God, yielding to the process and not getting stuck in the wilderness. Because of this success, the pastor wanted my husband and I to challenge the people of God to come up in their thinking because there is a sense of urgency for the saints to do *great* things in the Kingdom, and to allow God to use His children in the marketplace. We encouraged those who are called to occupy the mountain of business.

After we finished ministering, and while at the altar praying, prophesying, and laying hands on those who were in attendance, a shift in the atmosphere took place. A strong and undeniable holy heat fell in the church. We knew God was up to something great and wanted to do even more among the people.

The glory of God was so thick that it came in and rested on the house, even after we finished ministering. We all were in our seats humbled and thankful for the presence of God. I remember my husband looking at me and saying, "The people don't want to leave." Service had mostly been released, but the glory of the Lord was still resting strong in the building.

While I was ministering, I had felt fire on my face, mouth, hands, arms and feet. I had often read and heard how the Lord Jesus would appear in services and things would shift and change. There was be an increase in healing and deliverance when the King of Kings showed up.

We departed from the service still in awe of His glory. While driving home I kept asking my daughter Jayla, "What did you see? What did you see?"

Jayla will be referenced many times in this book because this is the child who was called at an early age as a seer-prophet. I later go into detail of her first expressed encounter with angels, but for now let me expound on this glorious experience with Jesus!

"What did you see?"

She didn't respond. I was trying not to get frustrated because I prophetically *knew* she had seen in the realm of the spirit. After asking a few times, she finally said, "Mommy, I'm going to write it down."

The following is what she saw during the service:

YES, JESUS WAS THERE. GLORY!

- Jesus was laying His hands on people's backs.
- The Lord's hands were touching heads sending sparks of light through them.
- The Lord's hands were releasing white dust over the people.

- The Lord's hands were sending loads of keys down.

- Two big and tall angels were standing on either side of the pulpit.

- Angels were in the seats attentive to the message (listening) while Daddy and Mommy were going forth in ministry.

As soon as we read Jayla's vision, we immediately called the pastors of the ministry. The pastor said that two minutes prior to our call he was telling his wife that he felt Jesus there, and he felt Jesus place His fist on his back. It was a "thrusting forth." He said, "I've never experienced anything like that before in my life."

During the service that night, the prophetic had come forth with such power. As we were closing out and I was about to pass the microphone over to the pastor to end our part of ministry, I looked over to the left and the Lord said to me, "Pray for the pastor!" I felt a strong pull to the man of God of the house. At first, I didn't want to go over to him. No matter how strong or anointed you are in the Lord, there are still times when you battle with fear—and especially because the glory was so thick, I *didn't* want to mess up anything, that holy fear and reverence. In the few seconds when the Holy Spirit and I were going back and forth and I was hearing, "Pray for the man of God," I suddenly told my husband we needed to pray for him.

As we walked toward him and started to pray and decree the Word of God over his life, he was pushed to the floor in a surrendered state, which was the same time Jesus was behind him thrusting him forth. The prophetic started to operate, but this time it was very bold. As I reflect back, I know beyond a shadow of a doubt there were angels also there assisting us in ministry.

It felt as if I was out of my body prophesying—as if I was there but not there. I know the angels were there assisting, as it felt like coals were placed on my mouth to prophesy from a heavenly realm.

He touched my lips with the burning coal and said, "This has touched your lips, and now your guilt is gone, and your sins are forgiven" (Isaiah 6:7 Good News Translation).

Fifteen years! Fifteen years! Fifteen years!

One of the phrases I heard was "Fifteen years," so I asked the woman of God how long they had been in ministry and she said, "Fifteen years!" God said that for every year they were in ministry, there would be a reward. There would be a Kingdom reward experienced and received on this side. God wanted them to know that the work of the Lord had not been in vain.

Such a sovereign move of God took place that night. Jesus was there unlocking, releasing, delivering—and I believe birthing. The angels were there assisting to make sure the plans of Heaven were established on earth. Glory to His holy name!

If you heard from the Lord to start a ministry, or you currently have a ministry, please be encouraged as the work He has called you to do is not in vain.

Therefore, my beloved brethren, be ye stedfast, unmoveable, always abounding in the work of the Lord, forasmuch as ye know that your labour is not in vain in the Lord (1 Corinthians 15:58 KJV).

Operating as Jesus operated during the service will allow you to tap into the abundance of what the Kingdom has. My husband and I aren't perfect. God knows we strive daily to live lives pleasing to Christ. I was so thankful this experience took place prior to the release of this book so I could include it to offer hope. When you intentionally do what is right according to the Word of God, even when you don't feel like it, heavenly portals are open and the glory of the Lord and His holy angels are released to demonstrate Kingdom power.

Angels played such an important part in the life of our personal Savior Jesus Christ when He was sent to the earth to perform the will of

God. Personally, I believe their presence is more important than many of us recognize.

ANGELS IN JESUS'S LIFE

Because Scripture reveals this fascinating part of angels being involved in the ministry of Jesus, why not believe they are also to be active and play important roles in our life, helping us to carry out God's plan for us?

Jesus lived a life of obedience. He lived a life of prayer. He lived a life of surrendering His will to the will of the Father—and angels played a huge part in His ministry.

Jesus is our King and our Redeemer! He is to be respected! He is to be reverenced! He is to be honored! Jesus is the Lord of hosts—the host of angels, the heavenly host.

> *Praise Him, all His angels; praise Him, all His hosts!* (Psalm 148:2).

Moments prior to Jesus's conception, leading up to His birth, and even unto His death, Scripture reveals that the holy angels were greatly involved during these times. After His burial and resurrection, more infallible proofs were recorded. We can learn a great deal about Jesus's interaction with angels as we take a closer look at the Scriptures. We can also gain knowledge and insight into the open heaven He created, which allowed miracles to be experienced and Heaven to respond.

Let's take a closer look at some pertinent times angels were involved according to the Holy Scriptures:

1. *The angel Gabriel predicted the birth of Christ to Mary.*

> *Then the angel said to her, "Do not be afraid, Mary, for you have found favor with God. And behold, you will conceive in your womb and bring forth a Son, and shall call His name Jesus. He will be great, and will be called the Son of the Highest; and the Lord God will give Him the throne of His father David.*

And He will reign over the house of Jacob forever, and of His kingdom there will be no end" (Luke 1:30-33).

2. Angels were present at the birth of Christ.

Suddenly a great company of the heavenly host appeared with the angel, praising God and saying, "Glory to God in the highest heaven, and on earth peace to those on whom his favor rests (Luke 2:13-14 NIV).

Many angels were there. There was a multitude, a great company of the heavenly host.

3. An angel warned Joseph about Herod's plot to kill Jesus.

After Herod died, an angel of the Lord appeared in a dream to Joseph in Egypt and said, "Get up, take the child and his mother and go to the land of Israel, for those who were trying to take the child's life are dead" (Matthew 2:19-20 NIV).

There was a natural "human" enemy and spiritual enemy involved. This Scripture reveals *why* it is so important to hear and obey Heaven's instructions.

4. Angels ministered to Christ after His temptation by the devil.

An angel from heaven appeared to him and strengthened him (Luke 22:43 NIV).

5. Angels were ready to help when Jesus was betrayed.

Do you think that I cannot appeal to My Father, and He will at once put at My disposal more than twelve legions of angels? (Matthew 26:53 NASB)

6. **An angel rolled back the stone from the tomb of Joseph of Arimathea.**

   There was a violent earthquake, for an angel of the Lord came down from heaven and, going to the tomb, rolled back the stone and sat on it (Matthew 28:2 NIV).

7. **An angel announced the resurrection of Christ.**

   But the angel said to the women, "Do not be afraid; I know that you are looking for Jesus who has been crucified. He is not here, for He has risen, just as He said. Come, see the place where He was lying" (Matthew 28:5-6 NASB).

8. **Christ ascended into Heaven with angels present.**

   While they looked steadfastly toward heaven as He went up, behold, two men stood by them in white apparel (Acts 1:10).

9. **The Bible says angels will be with Christ at His second coming.**

   He will send His angels with a great sound of a trumpet, and they will gather together His elect from the four winds, from one end of heaven to the other (Matthew 24:31).

10. **When Christ comes again, angels will execute His judgment.**

    And to give relief to you who are afflicted and to us as well when the Lord Jesus will be revealed from heaven with His mighty angels in flaming fire (2 Thessalonians 1:7 NASB).

11. **Angels will separate the righteous from the wicked.**

    The Son of Man will send out His angels, and they will gather out of His kingdom all things that offend, and those who practice lawlessness, …So it will be at the end of the age. The angels will come forth, separate the wicked from among the just (Matthew 13:41,49).

12. *After the separation of the unrighteous from the righteous, angels will hear Christ either acknowledging or denying each person.*

I tell you, whoever publicly acknowledges me before others, the Son of Man also will acknowledge before the angels of God (Luke 12:8 NIV).

It is a beautiful witness to know that the ministry of angels is found throughout the life of Christ. From His birth to His ministry call to His ascension into Heaven, the fact that angels had an attentive role in the ministry of Jesus is another testimony of His deity. Just as they surround the throne of God the Father and serve Him, they also were around Jesus while He was on earth. It should be very encouraging to know they are with you as well.

ADDITIONAL SCRIPTURE REVEALING ANGELS IN THE LIFE OF CHRIST

Now in the sixth month the angel Gabriel was sent by God to a city of Galilee named Nazareth (Luke 1:26).

- An angel announced the birth of John the Baptist; Luke 1:11-17.

- An angel foretold the name of John; Luke 1:13.

- An angel foretold to Mary the birth of Jesus; Luke 1:26-37.

- An angel foretold to Joseph the birth of Jesus; Matthew 1:20-21.

- An angel foretold the name of Jesus; Matthew 1:21.

- An angel announced to shepherds the birth of Jesus; Luke 2:8-15.

- Angels sang hallelujahs when Christ was born; Luke 2:13.

- An angel directed the Christ-child's flight into Egypt; Matthew 2:13,20.

- Angels ministered to Jesus following His three temptations; Matthew 4:11.

- An angel came to Jesus in Gethsemane; Luke 22:43.

- An angel rolled away the stone at His tomb; Matthew 28:2.

- An angel announced Jesus's resurrection to the women; Matthew 28:5-7.

- Two angels were in His tomb after the resurrection; John 20:11-14.

- Two angels were present at His ascension to Heaven. Angels will accompany His second coming; Acts 1:10-11.

One of my personal favorite Scriptures: "And there appeared an angel unto him from heaven, strengthening him" (Luke 22:43 KJV).

UNDERSTANDING THE CHARACTERISTICS OF JESUS

It is imperative to understand how Jesus walked. Since this chapter deals with angels and their interaction with Christ, I felt led to write about His attributes, which gives us a clear, visible understanding of how to keep heavenly portals open over our lives that we may on a regular basis experience the supernatural that angels bring with them.

Jesus walked in the *"fruit of the Spirit"* (Ephesians 5:22-23). Jesus mentions in His foundational teaching, the Sermon on the Mount, *"Blessed are the meek, for they shall inherit the earth"* (Matthew 5:5 KJV). The fruit of the Spirit is an excellent baseline of the way we as believers should operate. Since our Father outlined them in Scripture, it reveals the importance in the life of the believer, but more importantly, we can clearly see that our Lord and Savior operated in the fruit of the Spirit. Therefore, if our precious Lord and Savior exemplified these attributes, then how much more should we. Let us make a decision to do as He did.

Let's examine and explore each fruit described in Galatians 5:22-23:

But the fruit of the Spirit is love, joy, peace, longsuffering, kindness, goodness, faithfulness, gentleness, self-control. Against such there is no law.

- *Love* enables us to appreciate our brothers and sisters in the Lord, and, of course, our family and others around us. Love is taking the initiative to build up and meet the needs of others without expecting anything in return. See John 13:1; John 15:13; 1 Corinthians 13:3.

- *Joy* allows us to enjoy His creation, others, and our circumstances with an expression of delight and real authentic happiness from and with harmony with God and others. See Proverbs 15:13; John 15:11; John 17:13.

- *Peace* is surrendering and yielding to the Lord's control, for He is our ultimate peace! It is allowing tranquility to be our tone and to control our equanimity. This will be fueled by our harmonious relationship with God so we can hand over control of our heart, will, and mind to Him. Once we make real peace with God, we will be able to make and maintain peace with others. See Matthew 5:9; Colossians 3:15; Philippians 4:7.

- *Longsuffering, or patience,* is showing tolerance and fortitude to others, and even accepting difficult situations from them and God without making demands and conditions. See Matthew 27:14; Romans 12:12; James 1:3,12.

- *Kindness* is practicing benevolence and a loving attitude toward others. See Ephesians 4:32.

- *Goodness* displays integrity, honesty, and compassion to others and prompts us to do the right thing. See Matthew 19:16.

- *Faithfulness* is the "gluing" fruit that preserves our faith and the other characters of the Spirit as well as identify God's will, so we can be dependable and trusting to God and others. See 1 Corinthians 12:9; Hebrews 11:1; 1 Thessalonians 5:24.

- *Gentleness* is the character that shows calmness, personal care, and tenderness in meeting the needs of others. See Isaiah 40:11; Philippians 4:5; 2 Timothy 2:24; 1 Thessalonians 2:7. A gentle, or meek, person is willing to be submissive, humble, and relies on God and is dependent on Him to provide strength. See Isaiah 11:4; Matthew 5:5.

- *Self-Control* allows us to have discipline and restraint with obedience to God and others. See 1 Thessalonians 5:22.

More attributes and characteristics of Jesus Christ in addition to the fruit of the Spirit:

Forgiving is the realization of how much we have been forgiven by Christ. This enables us to forgive the insignificant things that are done to us. Forgiveness involves not being resentful of others and ignoring the wrongs that we have received so we can heal relationships by expressing Christ's love. See Luke 23:34; Ephesians 4:32; Colossians 3:13.

Humility minimizes arrogance and removes pride. It is understanding our fallen nature and tendency to think we are better than we are, and our striving to lift up ourselves above others and God. It is admitting that others, and more importantly God, is responsible for our achievements. Humbleness enables us to be a teachable person who is willing to have the attitude of submission and servanthood, and to be one who confesses sin and remembers how Christ served us. See Luke 22:27; Philippians 2:8; 1 Peter 5:3-5.

Friendship is the companionship and closeness we are to have with one another. It is the commitment to help form the character in others. This is not to be feared but embraced, even when it hurts. See Proverbs 27:17.

Honesty and Truthfulness mean being straight and honest with others and doing what is right. This trait allows us to earn trust by being accurate with facts and situations. See 2 Corinthians 8:21; Ephesians 4:25.

Purity and Holiness is being set apart for God's use, which is holiness in action. It does not allow us to be contaminated nor interfere with others in our growth and relationship in Christ. See Matthew 5:8; Philippians 4:8; 1 Timothy 1:5; 1 Timothy 5:22; James 4:8.

Confidence helps us rely on the Lord for all things in our life. It enables us to push forward in the direction that we are called because He is governing. Confidence makes us realize we are not responsible for the results—only the obedience. See Philippians 4:13.

Obedience is submitting to do what God requires of us. It is also recognizing the authority and direction from others, such as the pastor and church, so we can create winning situations. See Deuteronmy 13:4; Proverbs 19:16; John 14:14; John 15:14; 2 Corinthians 10:5.

Discipline is upholding and continuing a consistent and well-ordered life through godly obedience, regardless of how we feel. See 1 Timothy 4:7.

Jesus is our perfect example, our earthly role model to follow, and He gives us much hope that we can live lives without sin while accomplishing the will of God.

Other interesting characteristics of Jesus are found at the following website: http://seekthisjesus.com/60-character-traits-of-christ/.

ANOTHER VISION OF JESUS DURING SERVICE!

During one of our services, such glory began to fill the place. The gifts of the Spirit were in operation as tongues came forth with interpretation. As things began to come back down, I prophetically knew my daughter, Jayla, experienced a vision she was to share with the ministry. This is the same daughter I referenced previously; however, this was her first time seeing Jesus in a vision. While we were sitting down in service, I asked her what was she seeing, and as I grabbed her hand and took her before our pastors to share the vision, she said, "HE WAS HERE!"

Yes! Jesus showed up during a time of worship. She described His garment, stating He was wearing an all-white robe with royal blue on His garment. This was so impressive to me. The prophetic came forth and was powerful that day while in church. Later while I was in my seat, I heard the Lord say that He was visiting churches this morning. May we all create an atmosphere that allows Christ to step in.

Later that day my sister-in-love, Hope, sent me a text thanking me for pushing Jayla to share her vision. She also saw the same vision. She knew it was Jesus and she stated it was a beautiful confirmation of His love toward us. Seeing angels is the norm for Jayla, but again this was the first time she actually saw HIM—Jesus! Bless His holy name!

It is so important that we share our experiences as it gives us hope to keep pressing through painful situations. It gives us hope that His love toward us is so real. Jesus wants us to have these heavenly experiences. He desires to visit you, beloved. Don't close yourself off and don't block your heart. If you are a pastor or ministry leader, invite Jesus in to have tangible experiences with Him. These tangible manifestations are life changing, and I believe as we approach His return, we as a body will experience these encounters more and more.

I prophetically feel we are in a time when we are going to see, witness, and experience Jesus Christ coming out of Heaven and stepping right into our sanctuaries. He is going to destroy the work of darkness right at the altar. He is going to demolish the work of the enemy and

He is coming with His heavenly host so that the purpose of God may be fulfilled.

Throw away the Sunday programs and allow the Spirit of God to come in and have His way. Do not grieve Him. Do not quench Him.

Do not quench the Spirit (1 Thessalonians 5:19).

And do not grieve the Holy Spirit of God, by whom you were sealed for the day of redemption (Ephesians 4:30).

Just as the Holy Spirit can be grieved and quenched, so can our Lord and Savior Jesus Christ be quenched. Quench means: to put out; to terminate by destroying; to cause to lose heat or warmth. If we do not allow the Spirit to reveal Himself the way that He wants to, we are quenching Him.

Ask for the experiences! Ask for the visitations! Ask for the encounters! And open your heart to receive.

After Christ's death, burial, and resurrection, He appeared numerous times. Scripture tells us that He appeared to the apostles and He spoke to them concerning the Kingdom of God. He encouraged them to wait for the promise, which was the Holy Spirit coming with fire.

I've included this because if He decides to appear to you, it indeed is scriptural and it indeed is sound.

Then the eleven disciples went away into Galilee, to the mountain which Jesus had appointed for them. When they saw Him, they worshiped Him; but some doubted (Matthew 28:16-17).

Later He appeared to the eleven as they sat at the table; and He rebuked their unbelief and hardness of heart, because they did not believe those who had seen Him after He had risen (Mark 16:14).

Then, the same day at evening, being the first day of the week, when the doors were shut where the disciples were assembled, for fear of the Jews, Jesus came and stood in the midst, and

*said to them, "Peace be with you." When He had said this, He
showed them His hands and His side. Then the disciples were
glad when they saw the Lord* (John 20:19-20).

Upon my study regarding angels in the life of Jesus, I happened to
zone in on these Scriptures, which to me were very interesting.

One of the appearances was recorded in the book of Acts 1:8-11. The
two men who *"stood by them"* were angels, which shows their heavenly
task, heavenly assignments, and heavenly orders. As Jesus was ascending
and descending from Heaven to earth, so were the holy angels ascending
and descending with Him.

*"But you shall receive power when the Holy Spirit has come
upon you; and you shall be witnesses to Me in Jerusalem, and in
all Judea and Samaria, and to the end of the earth." Now when
He had spoken these things, while they watched, He was taken
up, and a cloud received Him out of their sight. And while they
looked steadfastly toward heaven as He went up, behold, two
men stood by them in white apparel, who also said, "Men of
Galilee, why do you stand gazing up into heaven? This same
Jesus, who was taken up from you into heaven, will so come
in like manner as you saw Him go into heaven"* (Acts 1:8-11).

I was in awe of this revelation. You may also be in awe of the glory
and majestic ways of our King. As you close out this chapter and read
the next chapter about God's holy angels, their functions and their protection in the lives of God's people, please be encouraged. No matter
what battles you are facing, continue to pull on Heaven—the answers
await you.

CHAPTER 2

THE MINISTRY OF ANGELS

ANGEL FEATHERS APPEARED

It was a Friday night, almost midnight, and I got out of bed to go to the restroom one last time before I went to sleep. And as I passed the bathroom mirror, I noticed something in my hair. My thoughts were, *Oh my, what's this?* As I looked more closely in the mirror, I noticed it was a white feather. *Wait! This is an angel feather!*

I remember rushing out of the bathroom and as I went over to my husband's side of the bed, I pointed to the feather in my hair and said, "Do you see this? There's a feather in my hair. This has to be an angel feather." Right after that, my husband jokingly said, "Well there is another one on the floor in the bathroom and it's been there since Wednesday." *Wednesday? And I haven't noticed it?*

Remember, this feather that appeared in my hair showed up around midnight on a Friday night. So, the first feather appeared, unbeknownst to me, two days prior. What really stood out to me was that the floor where the feather was had no rug. It happened to be in the bathroom stall where, ironically, I hadn't decorated. I say ironically because I love to decorate but the only things in this area were the toilet, toilet paper, and the blinds on the window.

When I found the feather in my hair, a little thought came to mind whether it could have been a feather from my pillow, because after all I was lying in bed before noticing it. But after this experience, two feathers released in a couple of days, I knew something was up and indeed it was.

From that time on, angel feathers started appearing on a regular and consistent basis.

Sometimes when I would go into my prayer room and then come out, a feather would be lying on the floor. Or I would go upstairs and look down on my hardwood floors and there would be a feather. There would be times when I would be cleaning the kitchen and feathers would be in the pile after sweeping, and I'd gracefully pick them up. Angel feathers kept appearing day after day! When they first started showing up, I was so happy and so excited and so thankful. I sent pictures and videos to my prayer partners in amazement of what God was doing because I knew there was a purpose to each and every feather that was released in my home.

My family quickly recognized that God was doing a great work and a piece of Heaven was showing up in our midst. The supernatural was merging with the natural, so much so, that it became a daily occurrence and experience. The Lord also allowed my family to experience the angel feathers—they were appearing to my daughters. When guests would visit our home, they started receiving feathers as well. Sometimes feathers would fall out of thin air and indeed there was no denying angels were nearby and it was Heaven's desire to allow us to experience their closeness.

I still don't know what happened or why God allowed me to experience this, but one particular day the feathers continually appeared; every time I would turn around, I saw one after another after another. I even remember videoing the feathers to share with my prayer partner—and during the video, yes, while recording the actual video, a feather fell out of thin air and into my hand. Tears came to my eyes as I begin to think about the goodness of Jesus and how He is so concerned about us!

OUR INTENTIONAL GOD

Because we serve an intentional God, I began to seek Him about these angel feathers. As mentioned earlier, angels have always been fascinating to me, but I knew there was a purpose in all of this. And that's when the questions started.

In some churches, people have been told not to ask God questions. But I believe that statement is far from the truth. You must ask questions; for when you do, the spirit of knowledge and wisdom will be given and granted.

God, why now? God, what's really going on? He impressed upon me that He wanted me to teach His people about angels. Though there have been other generals in the Kingdom who have written on this subject matter of angels, there is not nearly as much as there should be.

As stated in the Preface, I also believe the church has studied on demons and deliverance for far too long, allowing the teaching on angels to be minimized. A burden was placed on me that His desire is to restore hope to the body of Christ—believers—and increase the faith of many who are lost. The Spirit of the Lord began to show me that because of the lack of faith, many are not able to experience the supernatural miracles that should occur on a natural basis.

In addition, God started to impress upon me that it is very difficult to receive from Heaven when doubt and unbelief are the norm. *Bringing awareness of the supernatural not only softens our hearts but it also allows our hearts to open up to all of the possibilities that Heaven has to offer.* I've been teaching for a while that the supernatural should be natural in the lives of believers. It should be the norm; but the sad reality for most, it is not. God's grace and mercy endures forever; and when we believe in the supernatural, things begin to shift and change quickly around us.

The Lord also assured me that there was a purpose for all the feathers. One of the main purposes was to let me and my family know angels are with us, watching over us, and assisting us to carry out the God-given assignment over our lives. If that purpose holds true for me and my family, it definitely holds true for you and yours. He encouraged me to share our experiences and release revelation that was given and granted from the throne. He said that others' faith would be activated and they too would start receiving angel feathers, gems, and experiencing the supernatural.

We welcome the angels of the Lord into our home! We invite them! We pray and ask God to release them—and for many years during prayer I would commission the angels of the Lord to go fight, defend, and bring peace, and the words really caught up! In other words, my declarations started to manifest.

This is why it is imperative that you pray and speak the Word of God—this is *nonnegotiable* if you want to see Heaven and earth collide.

Something happens to us when we have a true encounter with God. It is not our job to pursue "the supernatural" over pursuing God, but I do believe as we set our hearts on tapping into the supernatural with a sense of purity, we will embark upon many mysteries that are often missed by a vast amount of believers.

This book highlights many angelic encounters and glorious experiences; some I have witnessed and some are from those near and dear to my heart. My prayers and hope are that the Father will create a burning desire in your heart to hunger and thirst more after Him, causing the supernatural to occur and become a reality and a natural part of your life.

So let's discuss angels!

WHAT IS AN ANGEL?

Definition: Angel, one who is sent. A messenger. God's agent. God's servants. Spirit beings.

Angels are beings who have greater power and ability than humans (2 Peter 2:11).

Angels exist in Heaven, or the spirit realm, which is a level of existence higher than the physical universe (1 Kings 8:27; John 6:38).

Angels are also referred to as spirits (1 Kings 22:21; Psalm 18:10).

The word "angel" is derived from the Christian Latin word *angelos,* itself derived from the Greek *aggelos,* which is a translation of the Hebrew word *malach,* a messenger or worker of God.

Angels are:

- God's host
- God's army
- God's messengers
- God's warriors
- God's protectors
- God's worshipers
- God's guardians
- God's exhorters
- God's agents
- God's servants

Warrior: A person engaged or experienced in warfare. A brave or experienced soldier or fighter.

Messenger: A person who carries a message or is employed to carry. A dispatch bearer in government or military service.

Army: A large organized body of armed personnel trained for war, especially on land. A large number of people or things, typically formed or organized for a particular purpose.

Protector: A person or thing that protects someone or something. A defender, preserver, bodyguard, guardian, guard, champion, watchdog, knight in shining armor, guardian angel, chaperone, escort, keeper.

Agent: A person who acts on behalf of another person or group. One who is authorized to act for or in the place of another: such as a representative.

ANGELS ARE INNUMERABLE

Jesus said, "Don't you realize that I could ask my Father for thousands of angels to protect us, and he would send them instantly?" (Matthew 26:53 NLT).

John wrote in Revelation, "Then I looked, and I heard the voice of many angels around the throne, the living creatures, and the elders; and the number of them was ten thousand times ten thousand, and thousands of thousands" (Revelation 5:11). This Scripture reveals that angels are innumerable.

WHEN WERE ANGELS CREATED?

Angels were created years and years and years ago—before God created the world. The Lord says in Job 38:4-7:

> *Where were you when I laid the earth's foundation? Tell me, if you understand. Who marked off its dimensions? Surely you know! Who stretched a measuring line across it? On what were its footings set, or who laid its cornerstone—while the morning stars sang together and all the angels shouted for joy?*

To me, what's most important isn't *when* He created the angels but *why* He created them.

WHY WERE ANGELS CREATED?

Simply put, angels were created because God wanted them. As you read further through this book, you will gain knowledge about some functions of angels, allowing you to gain more understanding of *why* they were created. You will also be encouraged to know that angels have a huge responsibility in assisting the Father with carrying out His purposes for humanity. Yes! Angels help carry out your life's God-given purpose.

> *For by Him all things were created that are in heaven and that are on earth, visible and invisible, whether thrones or dominions or principalities or powers. All things were created through Him and for Him* (Colossians 1:16).

> *You alone are the Lord; You have made heaven, the heaven of heavens, with all their host, the earth and everything on it, the seas and all that is in them, and You preserve them all. The host of heaven worships You* (Nehemiah 9:6).

> *Praise Him, you heavens of heavens, and you waters above the heavens! Let them praise the name of the Lord, for He commanded and they were created* (Psalm 148:4-5).

ROLES ANGELS PLAY

- Angels communicate God's message.
- Angels guard and protect.
- Angels observe you.
- Angels intervene.
- Angels encourage you.
- Angels deliver you.
- Angels are there during birth.
- Angels care for the saints at death.
- Angels help ministries.

- Angels bring healing.

- Angels bring deliverance.

- Angels bring messages.

- Angels bring direction.

- Angels bring provision.

- Angels bring wisdom.

- Angels bring victory.

- Angels bring insight.

- Angels bring clarity.

- Angels bring peace.

- Angels bring comfort.

- Angels bring strength.

- Angels bring answers to prayer.

- Angels release judgment.

- Angels engage in warfare.

- Angels assist with salvation.

- Angels bring understanding.

- Angels bring encouragement.

- Angels fight against the demonic.

- Angels help with your purpose/destiny.

- Angels help carry out the will of God.

- Angels assist when the prophetic is being released.

- Angels bring revelation of dreams and visions.

- Angels respond to repentance under God's command.

The following Scriptures are listed so you can see how significant the roles of angels are in the lives of God's people. When you need assistance from angels, you may be able to apply any of these Scriptures based upon the need present at the time. You will find much encouragement in many of these Scriptures that you may be able to apply to your life. God's holy angels are fighting for you, your family, and your loved ones. No matter how things look, apply the Word of God over your situation, for the angels are there to help during times of need.

These are not only verses you can stand on, but also *biblical examples* of angelic and divine intervention in the lives of God's people. If He did it for them, He can also do it for you! I've also compiled a list of Scriptures, included in the last chapter of the book, that serve as a quick resource to apply to your circumstances. In addition, you can use this section as a great tool and study for Bible teachings, Bible studies, and witnessing because it is indeed scripturally sound.

Angels Bring Protection

For he will order his angels to protect you wherever you go (Psalm 91:11 NLT).

See, I am sending an angel before you to protect you on your journey and lead you safely to the place I have prepared for you. Pay close attention to him, and obey his instructions. Do not rebel against him, for he is my representative, and he will not forgive your rebellion. But if you are careful to obey him, following all my instructions, then I will be an enemy to your enemies, and I will oppose those who oppose you. For my angel will go before you and bring you into the land of the Amorites, Hittites, Perizzites, Canaanites, Hivites, and Jebusites, so you may live there. And I will destroy them completely (Exodus 23:20-23 NLT).

And the Lord sent an angel who destroyed the Assyrian army with all its commanders and officers. So Sennacherib was forced to return home in disgrace to his own land. And when he entered the temple of his god, some of his own sons killed him there with a sword (2 Chronicles 32:21 NLT).

The Angel in the Fiery Furnace

Then Nebuchadnezzar came as close as he could to the door of the flaming furnace and shouted: "Shadrach, Meshach, and Abednego, servants of the Most High God, come out! Come here!" So Shadrach, Meshach, and Abednego stepped out of the fire. Then the high officers, officials, governors, and advisers crowded around them and saw that the fire had not touched them. Not a hair on their heads was singed, and their clothing was not scorched. They didn't even smell of smoke! Then Nebuchadnezzar said, "Praise to the God of Shadrach, Meshach, and Abednego! He sent his angel to rescue his servants who trusted in him. They defied the king's command and were willing to die rather than serve or worship any god except their own God. Therefore, I make this decree: If any people, whatever their race or nation or language, speak a word against the God of Shadrach, Meshach, and Abednego, they will be torn limb from limb, and their houses will be turned into heaps of rubble. There is no other god who can rescue like this!" (Daniel 3:26-29 NLT)

Angels Bring Messages

Then the angel said, "I am Gabriel! I stand in the very presence of God. It was he who sent me to bring you this good news! (Luke 1:19 NLT)

But the angel said, "Don't be afraid, Zechariah! God has heard your prayer. Your wife, Elizabeth, will give you a son, and you are to name him John. You will have great joy and gladness, and many will rejoice at his birth, for he will be great in the eyes of the Lord. He must never touch wine or other alcoholic drinks. He will be filled with the Holy Spirit, even before his birth. And he will turn many Israelites to the Lord their God. He will be a man with the spirit and power of Elijah. He will prepare the people for the coming of the Lord. He will turn the hearts of the fathers to their children, and he will cause those who are rebellious to accept the wisdom of the godly" (Luke 1:13-17 NLT).

Then the Lord opened Balaam's eyes, and he saw the Angel of the Lord standing in the way with His drawn sword in His hand; and he bowed his head and fell flat on his face. And the Angel of the Lord said to him, "Why have you struck your donkey these three times? Behold, I have come out to stand against you, because your way is perverse before Me. The donkey saw Me and turned aside from Me these three times. If she had not turned aside from Me, surely I would also have killed you by now, and let her live."

And Balaam said to the Angel of the Lord, "I have sinned, for I did not know You stood in the way against me. Now therefore, if it displeases You, I will turn back." Then the Angel of the Lord said to Balaam, "Go with the men, but only the word that I speak to you, that you shall speak." So Balaam went with the princes of Balak (Numbers 22:31-35).

Angels Bring Deliverance

Now behold, an angel of the Lord stood by him, and a light shone in the prison; and he struck Peter on the side and raised him up, saying, "Arise quickly!" And his chains fell off his hands. Then the angel said to him, "Gird yourself and tie on your sandals"; and so he did. And he said to him, "Put on your garment and follow me." So he went out and followed him, and did not know that what was done by the angel was real, but thought he was seeing a vision (Acts 12:7-9).

The angel of the Lord is a guard; he surrounds and defends all who fear him (Psalm 34:7 NLT).

Very early the next morning, the king got up and hurried out to the lions' den. 20 When he got there, he called out in anguish, "Daniel, servant of the living God! Was your God, whom you serve so faithfully, able to rescue you from the lions?" Daniel answered, "Long live the king! My God sent his angel to shut the lions' mouths so that they would not hurt me..." (Daniel 6:19-22 NLT).

Angels Bring Direction

Another biblical example of angels providing guidance is when an angel spoke to Philip telling him to go southward where he would meet an Ethiopian: "Now an angel of the Lord spoke to Philip, saying, 'Arise and go toward the south along the road which goes down from Jerusalem....' So he arose and went" (Acts 8:26-27).

Behold, I send an Angel before you to keep you in the way and to bring you into the place which I have prepared. Beware of Him and obey His voice; do not provoke Him, for He will not pardon your transgressions; for My name is in Him (Exodus 23:20-21).

An angel directed Abraham's servant in Genesis 24:1-7 to find a wife for his son. Abraham told him, "He shall send His angel before you and you shall take a wife for my son from there." The angel directed the servant straight to Rebekah.

Angels Bring Divine Intervention

At dawn the next morning the angels became insistent. "Hurry," they said to Lot. "Take your wife and your two daughters who are here. Get out right now, or you will be swept away in the destruction of the city!" When Lot still hesitated, the angels seized his hand and the hands of his wife and two daughters and rushed them to safety outside the city, for the Lord was merciful. When they were safely out of the city, one of the angels ordered, "Run for your lives! And don't look back or stop anywhere in the valley! Escape to the mountains, or you will be swept away!" (Genesis 19:15-17 NLT)

Angels Bring Encouragement

When Ahab got home, he told Jezebel everything Elijah had done, including the way he had killed all the prophets of Baal. So Jezebel sent this message to Elijah: "May the gods strike me and even kill me if by this time tomorrow I have not killed you just as you killed them." Elijah was afraid and fled for his life. He went to Beersheba, a town in Judah, and he left his servant there. Then he went on alone into the wilderness, traveling all day. He sat down under a solitary broom tree and prayed that he might die. "I have had enough, Lord," he said. "Take my life, for I am no better than my ancestors who have already died." Then he lay down and slept under the broom tree. But as he was sleeping, an angel touched him and told him, "Get up and eat!" He looked around and there beside his head was some bread baked on hot stones and a jar of water! So he ate and drank and lay down again. Then the angel of the Lord came again and touched him and said, "Get up and eat some more, or the journey ahead will be too much for you." So he got up and ate and drank, and the food gave him enough strength to travel forty days and forty nights to Mount Sinai, the mountain of God (1 Kings 19:1-8).

Angels Bring Strength

Coming out, He went to the Mount of Olives, as He was accustomed, and His disciples also followed Him. When He came to the place, He said to them, "Pray that you may not enter into temptation." And He was withdrawn from them about a stone's throw, and He knelt down and prayed, saying, "Father, if it is Your will, take this cup away from Me; nevertheless not My will, but Yours, be done." Then an angel appeared to Him from heaven, strengthening Him (Luke 22:39-43).

Angels Are Present During Childbirth

And she brought forth her firstborn Son, and wrapped Him in swaddling cloths, and laid Him in a manger, because there was no room for them in the inn. Now there were in the same country shepherds living out in the fields, keeping watch over their flock by night. And behold, an angel of the Lord stood before them, and the glory of the Lord shone around them, and they were greatly afraid. Then the angel said to them, "Do not be afraid, for behold, I bring you good tidings of great joy which will be to all people. For there is born to you this day in the city of David a Savior, who is Christ the Lord. And this will be the sign to you: You will find a Babe wrapped in swaddling cloths, lying in a manger." And suddenly there was with the angel a multitude of the heavenly host praising God and saying: "Glory to God in the highest, and on earth peace, goodwill toward men!" (Luke 2:7-14)

Angels Are Present During Death

Finally, the poor man died and was carried by the angels to sit beside Abraham at the heavenly banquet. The rich man also died and was buried (Luke 16:22 NLT).

Suddenly there was a great earthquake! For an angel of the Lord came down from heaven, rolled aside the stone, and sat on it. His face shone like lightning, and his clothing was as white as snow. The guards shook with fear when they saw him, and they fell into a dead faint. Then the angel spoke to the women. "Don't be afraid!" he said. "I know you are looking for Jesus, who was crucified. He isn't here! He is risen from the dead, just as he said would happen. Come, see where his body was lying. And now, go quickly and tell his disciples that he has risen from the dead, and he is going ahead of you to Galilee. You will see him there. Remember what I have told you." The women ran quickly from the tomb. They were very frightened but also filled with great joy, and they rushed to give the disciples the angel's message (Matthew 28:2-8 NLT).

Angels Assist with Healing

And the Angel of the Lord appeared to the woman and said to her, "Indeed now, you are barren and have borne no children, but you shall conceive and bear a son" (Judges 13:3).

Now there is in Jerusalem by the Sheep Gate a pool, which is called in Hebrew, Bethesda, having five porches. In these lay a great multitude of sick people, blind, lame, paralyzed, waiting for the moving of the water. For an angel went down at a certain time into the pool and stirred up the water; then whoever stepped in first, after the stirring of the water, was made well of whatever disease he had (John 5:2-4).

Angels Help Ministries

Are not all angels ministering spirits sent to serve those who will inherit salvation? (Hebrews 1:14 NIV)

Angels Assist with Provision

Then Jesus was led up by the Spirit into the wilderness to be tempted by the devil. And when He had fasted forty days and forty nights, afterward He was hungry. Now when the tempter came to Him, he said, "If You are the Son of God, command that these stones become bread." But He answered and said, "It is written, 'Man shall not live by bread alone, but by every word that proceeds from the mouth of God.'" Then the devil took Him up into the holy city, set Him on the pinnacle of the temple, and said to Him, "If You are the Son of God, throw Yourself down. For it is written: 'He shall give His angels charge over you,' and, 'In their hands they shall bear you up, lest you dash your foot against a stone.'" Jesus said to him, "It is written again, 'You shall not tempt the Lord your God.'" Again, the devil took Him up on an exceedingly high mountain, and showed Him all the kingdoms of the world and their glory. And he said to Him, "All these things I will give You if You will fall down and worship me." Then Jesus said to him, "Away with you, Satan! For it is written, 'You shall worship the Lord your God, and Him only you shall serve.'" Then the devil left Him, and behold, angels came and ministered to Him (Matthew 4:1-11).

He commanded the skies to open; he opened the doors of heaven. He rained down manna for them to eat; he gave them bread from heaven. They ate the food of angels! God gave them all they could hold. He released the east wind in the heavens and guided the south wind by his mighty power. He rained down meat as thick as dust—birds as plentiful as the sand on the seashore! He caused the birds to fall within their camp and all around their tents. The people ate their fill. He gave them what they craved (Psalm 78:23-29 NLT).

And the water in the skin was used up, and she placed the boy under one of the shrubs. Then she went and sat down across from him at a distance of about a bowshot; for she said to herself, "Let me not see the death of the boy." So she sat opposite him, and lifted her voice and wept. And God heard the voice of the lad. Then the angel of God called to Hagar out of heaven, and said to her, "What ails you, Hagar? Fear not, for God has heard the voice of the lad where he is. Arise, lift up the lad and hold him with your hand, for I will make him a great nation." Then God opened her eyes, and she saw a well of water. And she went and filled the skin with water, and gave the lad a drink (Genesis 21:15-19).

Angels Bring Peace

Then the angel said to them, "Do not be afraid, for behold, I bring you good tidings of great joy which will be to all people" (Luke 2:10).

Angels Bring Clarity, Strength, Understanding and Revelation

Only I, Daniel, saw this vision. The men with me saw nothing, but they were suddenly terrified and ran away to hide. So I was left there all alone to see this amazing vision. My strength left me, my face grew deathly pale, and I felt very weak. Then I heard the man speak, and when I heard the sound of his voice, I fainted and lay there with my face to the ground. Just then a hand touched me and lifted me, still trembling, to my hands and knees. And the man said to me, "Daniel, you are very precious to God, so listen carefully to what I have to say to you. Stand up, for I have been sent to you." When he said this to me, I stood up, still trembling. Then he said, "Don't be afraid, Daniel. Since the first day you began to pray for understanding and to humble yourself before your God, your request has been heard in heaven. I have come in answer to your prayer. But for twenty-one days the spirit prince of the kingdom of Persia blocked my way. Then Michael, one of the archangels, came to help me, and I left him there with the spirit prince of the kingdom of Persia. Now I am here to explain what will happen to your people in the future, for this vision concerns a time yet to come." While he was speaking to me, I looked down at the ground, unable to say a word. Then the one who looked like a man touched my lips, and I opened my mouth and began to speak. I said to the one standing in front of me, "I am filled with anguish because of the vision I have seen, my lord, and I am very weak. How can someone like me, your servant, talk to you, my lord? My strength is gone, and I can hardly breathe." Then the one who looked like a man touched me again, and I felt my strength returning. "Don't be afraid," he said, "for you are very precious to God. Peace! Be encouraged! Be strong!" As he spoke these words to me, I suddenly felt stronger and said to him, "Please speak to me, my lord, for you have strengthened me" (Daniel 10:7-19 NLT).

Angels Bring Insight and Understanding

He explained to me, "Daniel, I have come here to give you insight and understanding" (Daniel 9:22 NLT).

Angels Bring Revelation in Dreams and Visions

As he slept, he dreamed of a stairway that reached from the earth up to heaven. And he saw the angels of God going up and down the stairway. At the top of the stairway stood the Lord, and he said, "I am the Lord, the God of your grandfather Abraham, and the God of your father, Isaac. The ground you are lying on belongs to you. I am giving it to you and your descendants. Your descendants will be as numerous as the dust of the earth! They will spread out in all directions—to the west and the east, to the north and the south. And all the families of the earth will be blessed through you and your descendants. What's more, I am with you, and I will protect you wherever you go. One day I will bring you back to this land. I will not leave you until I have finished giving you everything I have promised you." Then Jacob awoke from his sleep and said, "Surely the Lord is in this place, and I wasn't even aware of it!" (Genesis 28:12-16 NLT).

Angels Bring Answers to Prayer

In Caesarea there lived a Roman army officer named Cornelius, who was a captain of the Italian Regiment. He was a devout, God-fearing man, as was everyone in his household. He gave generously to the poor and prayed regularly to God. One afternoon about three o'clock, he had a vision in which he saw an angel of God coming toward him. "Cornelius!" the angel said. Cornelius stared at him in terror. "What is it, sir?" he asked the angel. And the angel replied, "Your prayers and gifts to the poor have been received by God as an offering! Now send some men to Joppa, and summon a man named Simon Peter. He is staying with Simon, a tanner who lives near the seashore." As soon as the angel was gone, Cornelius called two of his household servants and a devout soldier, one of his personal attendants (Acts 10:1-7 NLT).

Angels Help Win Victories in Battles

Now because of this King Hezekiah and the prophet Isaiah, the son of Amoz, prayed and cried out to heaven. Then the Lord sent an angel who cut down every mighty man of valor, leader, and captain in the camp of the king of Assyria. So he returned shamefaced to his own land. And when he had gone into the temple of his god, some of his own offspring struck him down with the sword there. Thus the Lord saved Hezekiah and the inhabitants of Jerusalem from the hand of Sennacherib the king of Assyria, and from the hand of all others, and guided them on every side. And many brought gifts to the Lord at Jerusalem, and presents to Hezekiah king of Judah, so that he was exalted in the sight of all nations thereafter (2 Chronicles 32:20-23).

"For out of Jerusalem shall go a remnant, and those who escape from Mount Zion. The zeal of the Lord of hosts will do this." Therefore thus says the Lord concerning the king of Assyria:

"He shall not come into this city, nor shoot an arrow there, nor come before it with shield, nor build a siege mound against it. By the way that he came, by the same shall he return; and he shall not come into this city," says the Lord. "For I will defend this city, to save it for My own sake and for My servant David's sake." And it came to pass on a certain night that the angel of the Lord went out, and killed in the camp of the Assyrians one hundred and eighty-five thousand; and when people arose early in the morning, there were the corpses—all dead. So Sennacherib king of Assyria departed and went away, returned home, and remained at Nineveh (2 Kings 19:31-36).

So on a set day Herod, arrayed in royal apparel, sat on his throne and gave an oration to them. And the people kept shouting, "The voice of a god and not of a man!" Then immediately an angel of the Lord struck him, because he did not give glory to God. And he was eaten by worms and died. But the word of God grew and multiplied (Acts 12:21-24).

Angels Release Judgment

For out of Jerusalem shall go a remnant, and those who escape from Mount Zion. The zeal of the Lord of hosts will do this. "Therefore thus says the Lord concerning the king of Assyria: 'He shall not come into this city, nor shoot an arrow there, nor come before it with shield, nor build a siege mound against it. By the way that he came, by the same shall he return; and he shall not come into this city,' says the Lord. 'For I will defend this city, to save it for My own sake and for My servant David's sake.'" Then the angel of the Lord went out, and killed in the camp of the Assyrians one hundred and eighty-five thousand; and when people arose early in the morning, there were the corpses—all dead. So Sennacherib king of Assyria departed and went away, returned home, and remained at Nineveh. Now it came to pass, as he was worshiping in the house of Nisroch his god, that his sons Adrammelech and Sharezer struck him down with the sword; and they escaped into the land of Ararat. Then Esarhaddon his son reigned in his place (Isaiah 37:32-38).

Let them be like chaff before the wind, and let the angel of the Lord chase them. Let their way be dark and slippery, and let the angel of the Lord pursue them (Psalm 35:5-6).

The angel of the Lord came and sat down under the oak in Ophrah that belonged to Joash the Abiezrite, where his son Gideon was threshing wheat in a winepress to keep it from the Midianites. When the angel of the Lord appeared to Gideon, he said, "The Lord is with you, mighty warrior" (Judges 6:11-12 NIV).

And God sent an angel to Jerusalem to destroy it. As he was destroying, the Lord looked and relented of the disaster, and said to the angel who was destroying, "It is enough; now restrain your hand." And the angel of the Lord stood by the threshing floor of Ornan the Jebusite (1 Chronicles 21:15).

Angels Respond to Repentance

David built an altar to the Lord there and sacrificed burnt offerings and fellowship offerings. He called on the Lord, and the Lord answered him with fire from heaven on the altar of burnt offering. Then the Lord spoke to the angel, and he put his sword back into its sheath (1 Chronicles 21:26-27 NIV).

Angels and Salvation

In the same way, there is joy in the presence of God's angels when even one sinner repents (Luke 15:10 NLT).

Therefore, angels are only servants—spirits sent to care for people who will inherit salvation (Hebrews 1:14 NLT).

Praise the Lord, you angels, you mighty ones who carry out his plans, listening for each of his commands. Yes, praise the Lord, you armies of angels who serve him and do his will! (Psalm 103:20-21 NLT)

ANGELS—TERMINOLOGY, MEANINGS, AND DEFINITIONS

I thought it would be a good idea to include definitions of some of the words I've used while praying and calling upon the heavenly host. In addition, there are definitions pertinent to the topic at hand.

Dispatch: Send off to a destination or for a purpose. Deal with (a task, problem, or opponent) quickly and efficiently. The sending of someone or something to a destination or for a purpose.

Release: Allow or enable to escape from confinement; set free. Allow (something) to move, act, or flow freely. Remove restrictions or obligations from (someone or something) so that they become available for other activity. Allow (something) to return to its resting position by ceasing to put pressure on it.

Commission: An instruction, command, or duty given to a person or group of people. Task project, mission, undertaking, give an order for or authorize the production of something.

Orders: The arrangement or disposition of people or things in relation to each other. According to a particular sequence, pattern, or method. An authoritative command, direction, or instruction.

Command: Give an authoritative order. Have authority over; be in charge of (a unit). Be in a strong enough position to have or secure (something). A body of troops or a district under the control of a particular officer.

Encounter: Meet (someone) unexpectedly. Unexpectedly experience or be faced. Encounter or undergo (an event or occurrence).

Implore: To call or pray for earnestly, entreat. To call upon in supplication, beseech. To beg for urgently or anxiously.

Experience: Practical contact with and observation of facts or events.

Supernatural: Of a manifestation or event attributed to some force beyond scientific understanding or the laws of nature. Manifestations or events considered to be of supernatural origin.

Many times when I pray, I intentionally use these words to release God's angels on assignment and I highly encourage you to do the same. Speak the word over your circumstances! Angels will show up! Remember they *hearken* unto the Word of God.

> *Bless the Lord, ye his angels, that excel in strength, that do his commandments, hearkening unto the voice of his word. Bless ye the Lord, all ye his hosts; ye ministers of his, that do his pleasure* (Psalm 103:20-21 KJV).

Ally: A sovereign or state associated with another by treaty or league: one associated with another as a helper: a person or group that provides assistance and support in an ongoing effort, activity, or struggle.

ANGELS HEARKEN

Let's look at the definition of the word "hearken." Hearken means to:

- Give heed or attention to what is said; listen
- Give respectful attention
- Pay attention

Hearken: a primitive root; to prick up the ears, i.e., hearken: attend, (cause to) hear (-ken), give heed, incline, mark (well), regard. 1) to hear, be attentive, heed, incline (of ears), attend (of ears), hearken, pay attention, listen. Incline, attend (of ears), hearken, pay attention, listen

The Hebrew definition of hearken as defined in Strong's Concordance (7181); *qashab* (pronounced: kaw-shab'); a verb; to incline (ears), attend.

The Greek definition of hearken as defined in Strong's Concordance (5219); *hypakouo* (pronounced hoop-ak-oo'-o); a verb; to listen, to harken, as one who on the knock at the door comes to listen who it is (the duty of a porter); to harken to a command, to obey, be obedient to, submit to.

Angels hearken to:

- Carry out God's plans
- To do His will
- Carry out His orders
- Carry out instructions
- Carry out assignments

Angels are fascinating and majestic beings and have interesting and incredible characteristics. Let's explore.

ANGEL CHARACTERISTICS

- Angels are intelligent.
- Angels are wise.
- Angels are holy.
- Angels are meek.
- Angels are patient.
- Angels are joyful.
- Angels are modest.
- Angels are glorious.
- Angels are mighty.
- Angels are obedient.
- Angels have wills.
- Angels can be visible or invisible.
- Angels can operate in our realm.
- Angels travel very fast.
- Angels are immortal.

- Angels can sing.

- Angels can speak different languages.

Other Characteristics of Angels seen in Scripture can be found at this website: http://seekthisjesus.com/60-character-traits-of-christ/.

ANGELS ARE NOT TO BE WORSHIPED

When John the Revelator received the revelation about all that was to come he bowed down to worship the angel. But the angel said, "No, don't worship me. I am a servant of God, just like you and your brothers the prophets, as well as all who obey what is written in this book. Worship only God!" (Revelation 22:9 NLT).

> *Don't let anyone condemn you by insisting on pious self-denial or the worship of angels saying they have had visions about these things. Their sinful minds have made them proud* (Colossians 2:18 NLT).

The names of two angels are mentioned in the Bible—Michael and Gabriel. One of my friends had an angelic encounter with Uriel, a name mentioned in the book of Enoch; but for the sake of keeping this book scripturally sound according to the Old and New Testaments, I don't mention any other angel names outside of what the Bible reveals, other than keeping the writing of the angelic testimonies and encounters exactly as they are written.

MICHAEL

Michael in Hebrew means "who is like God." He appears to be the one who does battle. Michael battles against satan and his angels.

- Daniel 10:13 (NLT), "But for twenty-one days the spirit prince of the kingdom of Persia blocked my way. Then **Michael, one of the archangels**, came to help me, and

I left him there with the spirit prince of the kingdom of Persia."

- Daniel 12:1 (NLT), "At that time **Michael, the archangel** who stands guard over your nation, will arise. Then there will be a time of anguish greater than any since nations first came into existence. But at that time every one of your people whose name is written in the book will be rescued."

- Jude 9 (NLT), "But even **Michael**, one of the mightiest of the angels, did not dare accuse the devil of blasphemy, but simply said, 'The Lord rebuke you!' (This took place when Michael was arguing with the devil about Moses' body.)"

- Revelation 12:7-8 (NLT), "Then there was war in heaven. **Michael** and his angels fought against the dragon and his angels. And the dragon lost the battle, and he and his angels were forced out of heaven."

GABRIEL

Gabriel means "man of God" another meaning is "God is my strength." He appears to be one who carries messages. Gabriel is an archangel who appeared to Daniel as a man and gave him the meaning of a vision. In the New Testament, he appeared to Zechariah, who was serving in the temple, to announce the birth of his son John the Baptist. Six months later Gabriel appeared to Mary, informing her that she would be the mother of Jesus.

- Daniel 8:16, "And I heard a man's voice between the banks of Ulai, who called, and said, '**Gabriel**, make this man understand the vision.'"

- Daniel 9:21 (NIV), "While I was still in prayer, **Gabriel**, the man I had seen in the earlier vision, came to me in swift flight about the time of the evening sacrifice."

- Luke 1:19 (NIV), "The angel said to him, 'I am **Gabriel**. I stand in the presence of God, and I have been sent to speak to you and to tell you this good news.'"

- Luke 1:26 (NIV), "In the sixth month of Elizabeth's pregnancy, God sent the angel **Gabriel** to Nazareth, a town in Galilee."

Angels are referred to by different names, titles, and phrases in the Bible. Following is a list:

Angel of His presence: Isaiah 63:9 (NASB), "In all their affliction He was afflicted, and the **angel of His presence** saved them; in His love and in His mercy He redeemed them, and He lifted them and carried them all the days of old."

Angel of the Lord: Matthew 1:20 (NASB), "But when he had considered this, behold, an **angel of the Lord** appeared to him in a dream, saying, 'Joseph, son of David, do not be afraid to take Mary as your wife; for the Child who has been conceived in her is of the Holy Spirit.'" See also Luke 1:11; Acts 5:19; 8:26.

Angels of God: Genesis 32:1, "So Jacob went on his way, and the **angels of God** met him."

Archangels: First Thessalonians 4:16 (KJV), "For the Lord himself shall descend from heaven with a shout, with the voice of the **archangel**, and with the trump of God. And the dead in Christ will rise first."

Cherubim: Genesis 3:24, "So He drove out the man; and He placed **cherubim** at the east of the garden of Eden, and a flaming sword which turned every way, to guard the way to the tree of life."

Gabriel: Luke 1:19, "And the angel answered and said to him, 'I am **Gabriel**, who stands in the presence of God; and was sent to speak to you and bring you these glad tidings.'"

Heavenly host: Luke 2:13-14 (NIV), "Suddenly a great company of the **heavenly host** appeared with the angel, praising God and saying, 'Glory to God in the highest heaven, and on earth peace to those on whom his favor rests.'" See also Nehemiah 9:6; Colossians 1:16.

Michael: Jude 9 (NASB), "But Michael the archangel, when he disputed with the devil and argued about the body of Moses, did not dare pronounce against him a railing judgment, but said, 'The Lord rebuke you!'"

Morning Stars: Job 38:7, "When the morning stars sang together, and all the sons of God shouted for joy?"

Rulers and Authorities: Ephesians 3:10 (NIV), "His intent was that now, through the church, the manifold wisdom of God should be made known to the rulers and the authorities in the heavenly realms." See also Colossians 1:16.

Seraphim: Isaiah 6:2 (NASB), "Seraphim stood above Him, each having six wings: with two he covered his face, and with two he covered his feet, and with two he flew."

Watchers: Daniel 4:17 (NASB), "This sentence is by the decree of the angelic watchers and the decision is a command of the holy ones, in order that the living may know that the Most High is ruler over the realm of mankind, and bestows it on whom He wishes, and sets over it the lowliest of men."

YOUR GUARDIAN ANGEL

When we are born, we all given a guardian angel who is released from Heaven and returns to Heaven when we die our physical death. I've heard a few ministers of the gospel who made mention of this during their heavenly visitations.

In the next chapter I share a testimony of my grandmother's protection. After her visit with us, an angel feather was released in my home and the Lord spoke to me and said, "That was her guardian angel." One thing that was very unique for me was that the feather looked older. The

Lord impressed upon me that this angel had been on the earth protecting her for ninety years. Absolutely amazing!

Guardian means defender, protector, or keeper.

THE MINISTRY OF ANGELS

The ministry of angels wasn't new to me at all. When I surrendered my life to the Lord in 1997, the Spirit of the Lord began to take me on such a wonderful journey, revealing my calling, revealing who I was in Christ, who I was born to be. And then, that also, in turn, led me on a life of fasting and prayer.

My personal testimony and how I came to know Christ is found in the Introduction of this book. But around 2001, shortly after I gave birth to our third daughter we named Jayla, who has been and will be referenced various times in this book, that the ministry of angels became a normal part of my life. When she was a little baby, I would notice Jayla looking off somewhere, and I knew she was gazing at angels. I could tell that she was being entertained by angels. It was very vivid. She would look up beyond me, smiling a lot. When she was about three years old, she began to talk about the angels. At that point, although angels were beings I believed in, I started having more discussions about them. I also began to open my spirit to receive anything that God would show me—and that is when my eyes opened to supernatural experiences too. I started training my spirit to tap into the supernatural.

God allowed me to see angels. I wasn't seeing angels as some would say they see angels, in terms of seeing them clearly. For example, I didn't see exact colors or their facial features.

However, the way I saw them, I knew they were angels. At first, I would see them out of my peripheral vision. I would see a speck of light, or at times I would see a soft white silhouette turn or move with much grace. When I turned away and looked back, it was gone. And then I started seeing them in four corners of the bedrooms. As I went upstairs to our bedroom or to my daughter's bedroom, right in front of the window, I would see an angel. And then, when I would go back and look again, it was gone. These sightings were very short—a matter of a second or two when God was allowing or opening up my vision, then it would go away. I also noticed that most of the time the angels would stand near windows, entrance ways, and doors.

Then God allowed me to see His angels around His people. It wasn't this way with everyone, but God opened my eyes to see them hovering closely to some people. In fact, I remember one particular woman of God who came to my home for us to do business. When she walked in, I was overwhelmed by the angelic activity; as she walked into my home, all around her were angels. There must have been about eleven angels. They were positioned very near, very close to her, bunched up around her. They were floating. Their feet were not touching the ground. And so, in the spirit realm, I could see them floating gracefully behind her, around her. They were all white. Beautiful white silhouette beings. I also saw visions of them being very tall and some were taller than the people I saw them around or even behind the individuals.

I also believe one of the reasons my eyes were opened to the spirit realm was the fact that I had given birth to a prophet-seer. A seer is someone called by God to see and hear in the spirit. Because my daughter was seeing in the spirit and I was very open to the supernatural, I also started seeing in the spirit. I wholeheartedly believe the anointing is transferable. Speaking of which, as I later started sharing experiences of angels, angel feathers, and gems falling, those who were near started to experience the same.

TRANSFERENCE OF ANOINTING

My family, friends, and prayer partners started experiencing "angel feathers." I am convinced just as the anointing is transferable, your obedience and ministry gifts also affect others. My daughters, mother, nieces, sister, and other close family members, in addition to prayer sisters, all started to share their experiences with finding angel feathers as well.

I believe all it is, is *faith*. Faith to believe in the supernatural. Faith to believe God wants people around you to experience supernatural encounters. Faith to believe that any and everyone can tap into this place to receive from Heaven. Belief is so important! The more they would believe, the more their faith would be released to receive. I started receiving picture after picture after picture of different angel feathers being released to them.

I pray God will open you up to the supernatural and allow you to experience a piece of Heaven on earth. Don't be surprised when angel feathers start appearing.

PROPHETIC WORDS AND VISIONS CONCERNING ANGELS

One day we were in a service and our pastor saw a BIG angel come into the sanctuary. Right before she saw the vision:

> I heard the word "preparation." God has been and is preparing His Church like never before. He is preparing us to evangelize on a greater level.

> We are in the end times and the great awakening is occurring right now. The supernatural power of God shall be released upon this earth in a magnitude and way we have yet to see. The Spirit of the Lord has been impressing upon me to tell my people to GET READY! A part of experiencing this supernatural move of God that will take place in the earth is for His children to be prepared.

Preparation: The action or process of making something ready for use or service or of getting ready for some occasion, test, or duty. This definition reminds me of the ten virgins in Matthew 25, The Parable of the Ten Virgins. Five were prepared and five were not prepared! Five were wise and five were foolish!

Later in the book, I write about creating an open heaven. A major part of us getting prepared and staying ready is to assure we are always under an open heaven. We must stay awake, alert, present, and discern the seasons we are in currently.

This is surely a time when God's remnant shall rise like never before; and with the remnant, His holy angels will be right there helping to bring in the harvest.

PROPHETIC VISION—I SAW ANGELS AWAKENING PEOPLE

While in prayer one morning, I saw a vision of angels waking people up. It was an urgent call and I could feel that the body of Christ, the Church, had fallen into a slumber state. That is the way I can best describe it.

During this time, I kept hearing "Rise up. Rise up." God is calling His children to rise up in the things of God and carry out their God-given assignments.

I heard the word "occupy." The definition of *occupy* is to engage the attention or energies of...; to take up (a place or extent in space).

My thoughts were, *Lord is Your Church ASLEEP?* God then started to lay it on my heart that many breaches have occurred in the spirit realm from His people being out of place, out of position, out of alignment, getting distracted by worldly things, backsliding, and falling into a state of complacency and compromise.

There was an inward witness that God was releasing His holy angels to start waking up His Church to assist with accomplishing His plans. The word shall come to pass and prophecy will play out before our very eyes.

We have work to do!

We have assignments to complete!

We have battles win!

We have to win souls!

YOU have work to do!

YOU have assignments to complete!

YOU have battles to be won!

YOU have to win souls!

> *We must work the works of Him who sent Me as long as it is day; night is coming when no one can work* (John 9:4 NASB).

I want you to write down a list of things you feel the Lord is telling you to do. Write them down now and date each one. Pray over the words you've written and begin to decree and declare.

_____

_____

_____

_____

_____

_____

_____

_____

_____

_____

_____

As we move forward, taking a look at our precious Lord and Savior Jesus Christ and the engagement and importance of these holy beings, it serves as a reminder of our need for them in our lives to help carry out the will of God concerning us.

CHAPTER 3

ANGELS AND PROTECTION

There is no doubt in my mind angels have helped protect and have saved countless lives since the creation of humanity. If our eyes were open to the supernatural realm on a regular basis, I'm sure there would be millions upon millions of stories about some sort of divine intervention from the smallest things such as an angel preventing a person from tripping and falling down to the prevention of drastic destruction sparing numerous lives.

I wholeheartedly believe there is an inner knowing that lies in all of us whether we want to believe it or not that angels have provided protection many times in our lives. If we stop and pause a moment and allow time of reflection of our years of existence, we may be able to look back with certainty and confess that some sort of divine being protected us from danger. I'm sure many would say there were times when their entire situation could have gone a totally different way.

I will never forget this following story. As I recall, I know beyond a shadow of a doubt angels were with the four of us that night. I was a little girl traveling with my mother and my two siblings, my oldest sister and brother. We were returning home, and for some reason, right before entering onto the interstate highway, Mom's car shut off. This was out of the blue with no prior signs of car trouble. My mother managed to drift into a parking lot near the traffic light where the car suddenly stopped. As we sat in the car in the parking lot for what seemed to be around thirty to forty-five minutes wondering what could be wrong with the car, an uncanny peace was released over us, so we just sat patiently and waited.

During our time of waiting, my mother tried to start the car, but to no avail. The car didn't crank, so we continued to wait. Finally, she was able to start the car and back on the road we went. As we entered onto the Interstate, we noticed traffic backed up. We could see in the distance ambulances, police cars, and vehicles piled up. As we made our way through the traffic, we eventually passed the scene of the accident and there were bodies lying on the ground—some had already been covered up as fatalities.

Why did my mother's car suddenly stop? Why were we not allowed to move anywhere as we found ourselves sitting in the middle of a parking lot? Could it be that grace was released on our behalf that day and God sent His holy angels of protection to save and spare our lives by delaying us from getting onto the interstate? Lives that could have been caught in the dangerous path of destruction due to a pile up of cars that resulted in a devastating accident? If you would have asked me these same questions as a young child, I would not have be able to adequately respond; however, now having understanding about our Father's heavenly host, I know beyond a shadow of doubt angels were present and delayed us from getting onto the dangerous interstate and protected our lives. To God be the glory!

Lord, we thank You for Your holy angels. We praise You, Lord, for releasing these holy creatures in our midst to fight battles, wage war, and protect us from the invisible and visible things that come up against us—protecting us from dangers seen and unseen.

On many of occasions I stood on Psalm 91, not realizing the validity of the words encompassed in the holy Word of God. There were times these words would burst out of my spirit and proceed out of my mouth and as I look back on the awareness of angelic and divine protection. I now have a deeper knowledge and sense that the Holy Spirit was speaking through me in many of those instances. We will never know the amount of angelic protection that has been released, but we all can rest assured that during many situations God's holy angels were fighting battles for us unimaginable.

More angelic encounters and testimonies will be shared in the Amazing Angelic Encounters chapter. These stories will encourage you through knowing the protection God's angels provide. As you read the following Scripture verses and stories, allow your heart to be opened and encouraged.

> *For He will give His angels charge concerning you, to guard you in all your ways* (Psalm 91:11 NASB).
>
> *The angel of the Lord is a guard; he surrounds and defends all who fear him* (Psalm 34:7 NLT).
>
> *Let them be as chaff before the wind, and let the angel of the Lord chase them* (Psalm 35:5).
>
> *Make their path dark and slippery, with the angel of the Lord pursuing them* (Psalm 35:6 NLT).

GOD PROTECTED MY DAUGHTERS AND NIECES

My husband, Gregg, and I decided to go home to Virginia to spend the 4th of July holiday with our family. We took the three youngest girls with us while our three oldest daughters—two being teens and one a young adult—along with their first cousins all packed up and headed to Georgia for a cousin vacation and getaway.

I believe it was the second day of the trip when we received word that things were not going so well for the girls; spiritually that is. While Gregg and I were in bed asleep in our hotel room, I was awakened in the middle of the night, approximately 1:30 a.m., by what sounded like four to five LOUD knocks. When I woke from a deep sleep, I inwardly knew that angels were waking me up. I felt them getting my attention and calling me to PRAY, and pray with urgency.

As I begin to intercede and pray in the spirit, immediately there was a knowing that the girls were in trouble, spiritual trouble that is. I also smelled smoke in the spirit realm and I felt a hell portal open over them. It was a very deep, dark demonic portal. I stayed in bed covering and praying for them and then I drifted off to sleep.

When morning came, my husband and I and our family called a prayer meeting via a conference call to have prayer with all of the girls. As they shared the different experiences and attacks they witnessed, we were more prepared and armored up—and we all went in, intercession and war tongues. One of my nieces shared that she looked at the clock while thinking about some of the things that transpired and it was 1:30 in the morning, the same time an angel woke me up to pray!

I will refrain from sharing all of the drastic details, but all seven girls witnessed and had seen in the spirit realm very dark, demonic, tormenting spirits. After our family prayed, things broke up in the atmosphere and the next day they experienced a peaceful day.

The following testimony was written by our daughter Jayla who witnessed the tallest angel she had ever seen in her life. My sister-in-love Tonya also saw an angel standing in front of the door with a sword in his hand ready for battle. This angel was standing in position guarding one of the doors. It turns out our niece had a roommate who had opened herself up to the other side, the dark side. When the girls arrived at her place for vacation, the anointing they carried stirred up the demonic as they all are saved and born again. Shortly after this happened, the roommate left and transitioned to another location, but we praise God and give glory to the Lord for protecting the girls during this time.

THREE-STORY TALL ANGEL TESTIMONY
by Jayla Scott

At this time I was on vacation with my older cousins and prior to me seeing the angel, we had been going through a series of attacks brought on by the enemy. The night before was the worst of all as each one of us was being attacked during the very early hours of the morning. There were many unwanted and misunderstood emotions brought on because of this.

But the next day after all that had happened, was one of the most glorious days that each of us had experienced. On this particular day, we decided to spend the day at the pool. Long story short, it felt as the night of torment never happened. There was so much peace and so much tranquility within the atmosphere. All of the troubles that we had gone through weren't forgotten but rather pushed to the very back of our minds.

When I saw the angel, my cousins and I were on the phone with our mothers recounting the troublesome events as they called to check up on us. We were sitting by the poolside, some of us were sitting on the cement with our feet in the pool, and others were in the pool. But we were gathered close so we could all listen to what was being said and all be heard when we spoke. At some point during the phone conversation, I glanced over to another side of the pool, and there was the angel—as tall as a three-story building. I knew in my spirit it was Michael, the archangel. He was a peachy orange color and had a very strong stance, demeanor. Thank You, Jesus!

ANGEL TESTIMONY
by Jazmine Marshea Scott (my oldest daughter)

God has perfect timing. First, I want to talk about how, in the summer of 2016, my relationship with God really started to develop. During that time is when my ears started becoming even more sensitive to His voice and my eyes began to open like never before. My discernment was significantly increased, and I started receiving many downloads from Heaven. My knowledge and understanding of certain things and how certain things work in the spirit realm began to increase as well. However, with that being said, I was honest with myself and I told God, "Lord, I know seeing in the spirit is a gift from You and I feel that You gave it to me, but I'm not ready for that right now. I'll stick with my discernment and whatever else for now, but I'm not ready for that." So for a time He certainly did honor that prayer of mine. As time went on, I was honest with myself again and told Him that I was ready to see in the spirit.

One encounter I had is when I went on my first date with the person I'm in a relationship with now, Dontá Davis (now fiancé). Before we met up that evening, I prayed to God for protection that His will be done, and that He would be with us during the date. While on the date, we were sitting outside talking, and in the midst of our conversation Dontá said, "I'm feeling wind behind my head. Do you feel that? What is that?" I immediately knew what it was but I didn't want to just come out and say, "Oh, it's just an angel behind you flapping its wings." But that is exactly what it was. I don't know what the angel actually looked like because I "see angels" as a knowing or through discernment. It's not necessarily always the same as seeing a human being. Rather, it's feeling a presence and discerning that an angel is near, as opposed to an evil spirit or demon.

Another way I have seen angels are as flashes of light. The light will be in my peripheral vision and only for a quick second. I'll see a flash and discern that that was an angel. The third way I see angels is when I'm asleep, but my spirit is still awake. I'm not fully conscious or awake; however, my spirit is conscious and it can see. So, I'm in between the conscious and unconscious realm. I can still see what's going on around me, but it's like I'm seeing into the spirit realm. This third way is how I have experienced my other angel encounters.

When I moved into my first home, I remember there was a lot of praying beforehand, praying for protection. I even went to the house before I was able to move in, and prayed that God would fill the space with His angels and presence. The way the house is designed, when walking through the front door, you can look up and see upstairs. My first night in the house, I walked in and saw an angel in a corner right upstairs. It had flashed and then it just went away. I was thinking,

Okay, did I really just see that? And I was happy because I knew I wouldn't be as nervous about staying there for the first time by myself. I thought, *Okay, good. I'm not here by myself. I'm not alone."*

Another encounter happened when I was at home sleeping in my bed, and as mentioned before about the different ways I see angels, I was in between realms. My spirit was awake and I remember looking off to the side and there was some Buddha-head thing hiding in a decoration I have in my bedroom staring at me. I'm thinking, *What is that? What are you doing here? Why are you looking at me?* Then I remember looking around the room to see what else was going on, and on both sides of my bed stood two angels facing each other. What I saw were two translucent figures with a superman-shape outline standing still like soldiers on each side of my bed. Despite seeing the Buddha-head thing first, I immediately felt a peace when I saw the angels, so I went back to sleep. The next morning while making my bed, I found an angel feather right in front of where one of the angels was standing.

Another angelic encounter I had was again with my fiancé Dontá when he invited me to the church he was attending. We didn't go there together. I went with my cousin and he went with some of his college teammates. Dontá and I weren't in communication with each other about when we would arrive at the service because we came with other people and didn't plan to sit together. But we did plan to meet up after the church service was over. I arrived a little bit earlier than he did and my cousin and I went ahead and found a seat.

For some reason, I felt Dontá's presence when he walked in. It's hard to explain. I felt it on my left side and I could feel like tingling or something inside like my spirit or soul was happy and recognized something. I said, "God, what is that?" He said, "Dontá is here." I looked over my left shoulder and Dontá was on the side, seated a few rows behind me. My thought was, *Okay, that was a little weird.*

Later I asked Dontá a few questions to confirm when he arrived as opposed to when I got there. Then I began trying to explain to him what happened and he's trying to understand, but he couldn't fully understand because I didn't even understand what happened at the time. While I was explaining to him the feeling and what happened during service, three angels appeared right in front of us. They were flashes of light that suddenly appeared and then just went away.

In some of the pictures that Dontá and I have taken, angel orbs have appeared after the fact. They show up in the pictures as circles. And a few times while Dontá and I were on FaceTime or talking on the phone, in the midst of our conversation, angels would fly up in front of me and then just go away. This happened on many different occasions, over ten times.

As my daughter shared this testimony, I believe angels were sent as a sign to show them that their union was ordained by God. Since Jazmine was a young child, I've prayed for her husband. Currently, we are in the process of planning their wedding—to God be the glory!

ANGEL TESTIMONY
by Erica Jeffers

Once or twice a year, a ministry I'm involved in goes to Moravian Falls, North Carolina, for spiritual retreats. Moravian Falls is a place in the mountains that is saturated with God's glory because there was prayer literally taking place for twenty-four hours, seven days a week for more than 100 years. This is also a place where angels have been spotted and several of us from our team would see them from time to time in and around our worship services.

At our retreats, we would always have powerful prayer walks on Saturday mornings. During one particular retreat, we ex-perienced one of our most powerful encounters "together." We would usually gather and pray in different locations around the prayer mountain. That morning we were at the foot of the mountain praying and worshiping, and we began to sing the hymn, "Holy, Holy, Holy." The presence of God enthroned us in such a mighty way that it was almost impossible to stop singing and worshiping Him.

As we began to walk back to the place where we were lodging, still basking in the glory of God, all of a sudden, each of us, one by one began gazing into the trees as we were all captivated by an iridescent glow that started small, but grew and grew into a massive substance that appeared to us to be soldiers march-ing in complete formation while coming into our dimension. It was an amazing sight to see, but even more amazing is that we all saw it and sensed the same thing at the same time. There was an overwhelming sense of peace and protection that I had never experienced before. It was apparent that God's heavenly host was and is encamped all around us.

Since this time, I've seen feathers in seemingly strategic places that remind me of the experience we had. One particular time is when I felt the Holy Spirit leading me to open my front door, for no apparent reason. After I opened the door, I looked down and there on my welcome mat was an angel feather. Be encouraged, beloved, our Father has dispatched His heavenly host to protect His children and to intervene on our behalf at the beckoning of His Word. May the eyes of our hearts be opened to see!

TORNADO CHANGED COURSE— ANGELIC PROTECTION

Devi Jhaneen wrote the following testimony:

You and Gregg weren't home, but the girls were. They were alone. We heard about the tornado in your part of town and you asked us to pray for your babies. I prayed and prayed. And I saw your girls in a bathroom. One was really, really, really scared. She was crying uncontrollably. But then an angel appeared outside your home. The angel was taller than your house with broad shoulders, with a beautiful gold bow and arrow on his back. He never reached for it, though. He spread his wings as if he was going to take flight. They were huge and formed a wall of feathers around the side of the house facing the tornado. Then he looked toward the tornado, gently, barely, parted his lips and started to blow…and the tornado instantly changed its course.

That testimony was mind blowing, as the terrible storm in our city wasn't the norm. Unbeknown to me, it would hit during a time my husband and I were away from the home—and our six daughters were at home by themselves. Our oldest daughter Jazmine was in charge. She was sixteen years old and responsible for taking care of the home and her sisters.

While I was in a meeting and Gregg was at his parents' home helping them, a dangerous storm was bearing down in our area. A storm that had not been this severe in years. While we were at the meeting that day, the power was going on and off sporadically—but we had no clue what was taking place outside the meeting place. When I learned of the storm, I decided to leave and go home. While driving home in the pouring rain, I thought, *This surely looks and feels different. This doesn't feel like the storms I'm used to seeing.*

As I got closer to home, I noticed what seemed to be tornado marks and paths created when tornadoes touch down, and there was much damage done to many areas where I passed by. As all of this is occurring, I remember calling my husband, asking him if he was aware of the severity of the storm and what was happening in our city. He assured me all would be well and he was on the way home. On that day a tornado outbreak had hit our state, an outbreak that took its toll on communities, schools, neighborhoods and, unfortunately, lives. Some people perished in this storm as trees fell on cars and homes. I can go on and on about this event; but I will say this, God assigned His holy angels to us and our home to watch over our precious girls that day.

One thing about that day really stands out for me. While I was getting dressed and getting ready that morning, I kept hearing the Lord say, "Cover the home and pray." There was an overwhelming push to get on my knees before I left our home and pray. I didn't pray for a long time, but I do remember covering my family and praying Psalm 91. The level of urgency was indescribable, so I obeyed. I got on my knees on my side of the bed and I prayed.

I host a "prayer call" and on the Monday following the storm and the aftermath, we all were sharing our testimonies. Then Devi saw the vision of what took place, the vision she shared a few paragraphs prior. Such a praise went out on that prayer call; with tears streaming down my face, I was reminded of the urgency to pray! The angel of the Lord came and not only protected my girls, but it blew one of the tornadoes in another direction. I believe that tornado would have come right through our neighborhood.

As I turned into my subdivision that day, I was so thankful that no damage was done and there was a feeling of "covering" that I would later discover why. As I look back, there was a peace over our entire neighborhood in the midst of everything that had broken out around us. The next day my husband and I went to get food due to power outages and about a half mile from our home, a tornado had destroyed much of everything in sight. Yes, only *a half mile* away from where we lived. Glory to God as He protected our daughters on a day that would go down in history. Praise the Lord!

GRANDMA AND HER GUARDIAN ANGEL

My grandmother had arrived from Chicago to North Carolina to visit us for Jazmine's (our firstborn) college graduation. She stayed with us for about a week and we had a beautiful time in the Lord. While with us, she pretty much sat in the same chair during the day. She would come down from the bedroom for the day, sit in the same place, and in the evening she would head to bed.

When it was time for her to return to Chicago, of course we prayed for safe travels. Shortly after the time when Grandma's flight was scheduled to land, we called to make sure she safely arrive. My older sister Tanya was on the phone talking to Grandma who said it was raining pretty bad in Chicago and that our cousin had picked her up as planned. Then all of a sudden Grandma shouted, "KATINA" and then nothing. The phone was still connected but there was no communication, which really scared my sister who turned to me and said, "I wonder if they were in an accident."

A few minutes later we received a call back that sure enough, they were involved in a bad car accident that totaled my cousin's car but *thank the Lord* they were safe. I immediately sent a prayer and intercession call to the intercessors I am connected with and they were praying as they took Grandma to the hospital via an ambulance. All ended up as well as expected, but then it got interesting.

The next morning, right after I finished the 5:30 a.m. prayer call, I was headed into my kitchen to prepare breakfast for my youngest daughters and a very different colored feather appeared right in the same exact spot where Grandma sat during her entire stay with us. For some reason, I recorded it on my phone, for the public to see which was not the norm, as I just began sharing some of my angelic feather experiences. But I didn't pay attention while I was doing the video, that this feather appeared right where Grandma had been sitting during her visit. Later that day as my sister and I were talking and thanking God for His protection, we realized that God was telling us, *This feather was sent as a sign that I was with your grandmother and family, and I protected them for the accident could have been worse.* We started thanking the Lord and praise filled our hearts! Another revelation God showed me was that this was our grandmother's guardian angel's feather.

As I stated earlier, the color of this feather was different; it wasn't as white as the feathers I normally saw, it looked like an older feather. There was an inner knowing that this angel had been on this earth protecting Grandma for ninety years. WOW! When I received that revelation, I was blown away. It was a slightly off-white color and its shape to me was more structured and defined. God allowed her angel to protect my family that day and I also believe prayer played a huge part in the outcome.

ANGEL PROTECTION WHILE SPEAKING ON THE COURTS OF HEAVEN

My husband and I had recently gone to the "courts of Heaven" as we were experiencing a high level of warfare that needed immediate attention.

After we went to the courts, I felt by the Spirit of the Lord that we were to take Jayla, our daughter, with us the next time we went. The Lord showed me she was given grace and access to go. The same day I shared with her our experience and also told her what the Lord said regarding her having access to go to the courts of Heaven.

Two days later after church, we called her into our bedroom because she wanted to share with us a dream she had regarding the courts of Heaven. The very same night after I told her she was granted access by the Lord, she said she had a dream and she saw the courts of Heaven. She described it the same way it was described by others in the book on the courts of Heaven. She saw brown and a lot of gold and she saw a large circular shape. She stated there were many, many books and she saw people there. She also saw one of her family members, who passed away a few years ago, smile and walk right past her. We know by the Spirit of God this family member made it into Heaven because he was saved.

The Lord was revealing to all of us, my husband, her, and me, that He was speaking and again she had access. He was speaking so much so that He allowed her to transcend the same night after our initial conversation. Now this is where things get a little interesting; she didn't tell me this the day it transpired, she told me awhile after it occurred.

While we were in our bedroom, she said she saw in the spirit realm a demon trying to choke me around my neck as I was talking about the courts of Heaven. She said, "As this thing was trying to choke you, Mommy, I saw four angels come and stand right behind you and it left." This reminds me of the word when it is sown the enemy tries to come and steal it immediately. "And these are the ones by the wayside where the word is sown. When they hear, Satan comes immediately and takes away the word that was sown in their hearts" (Mark 4:15). Praise God for His protection!

I highly recommend Robert Henderson books as I have received more revelation on this area, if you have not studied the courts of

Heaven. When I read his first book, the Holy Spirit immediately said this is end-time revelation released to His church.

CHILD SEES JESUS AND TWO ANGELS

This is such a beautiful testimony shared by one of my dear friends whose son, Justin Ugwuegbu, had a vision of Jesus and the angels:

> I'm Justin and I am ten years old. I had an encounter with Jesus when I was eight years old. I was sleeping and I had a dream that woke me up. I walked out to go to my mom and dad's room and I turned on the light because it was really dark. When I was turning the corner to go down where the stairs are, I looked downstairs and I saw something. I knew it was Him—Jesus. Jesus standing there and there were two angels, one on each side of Him with flaming swords. He wasn't there for a long time, so I kept waiting and it disappeared. Then I went to my mom's room and told her all about it.

CALLING ON MICHAEL THE ARCHANGEL

I saw my spirit out of my body. I was dressed in white. As I lay in my prayer room during the night, I was awakened to realize my spirit was in a war. What kind of war? I'm not sure but what I saw was my spirit was violently calling on Jesus; and as I called upon Jesus a few times, I asked Him to send Michael to war on my behalf. Right after that, I immediately woke up back in my body. I believe the Lord allowed me to witness that to make me aware of the fact that our spirit is as real as our body and that our spirits are always awake, alert, fighting, and battling even when we are sleep or are not aware that our spirits are doing such things.

OPEN OUR EYES, LORD

In Second Kings 6:8-23, the Bible describes how God provides an army of angels leading horses and chariots of fire to protect the prophet Elisha and his servant; God opens the servant's eyes so he can see the angelic army surrounding them. Here's a summary of the story, with commentary:

Syria was at war with Israel, and the king of Aram was disturbed by the fact that the prophet Elisha was able to predict where Aram's army was planning to go, and passed that information along to Israel's king in warnings so the king could plan the Israeli army's strategy.

Aram's king decided to send a large group of soldiers to the city of Dothan to capture Elisha so he wouldn't be able to help Israel win the war against his nation.

Verses 14 and 15 in Second Kings 6 (NIV) describe what happens next:

> *Then he sent horses and chariots and a strong force there. They went by night and surrounded the city. When the servant of the man of God got up and went out early the next morning, an army with horses and chariots had surrounded the city. "Oh no, my lord! What shall we do?" the servant asked.*

Being surrounded by a large army with no way to escape terrified the servant, who at this point in the story could only see the earthly army that came to capture Elisha.

The story continues in verses 16-17:

> *"Don't be afraid," the prophet answered. "Those who are with us are more than those who are with them." And Elisha prayed, "Open his eyes, Lord, so that he may see." Then the Lord opened the servant's eyes, and he looked and saw the hills full of horses and chariots of fire all around Elisha."*

Just as it is was with Elisha, many times we are fighting battles and going through circumstances where we may not even realize God is on our side every step of the way fighting our battles. If our eyes could be opened, we would see His mighty army of angels assisting us and bringing in the victorious win! Be encouraged.

Be it stories in the holy Scriptures that reflect the mercy and grace of God allowing angels to be sent forth recusing and protecting, or stories from individuals who have witnessed firsthand accounts of angels providing protection—make no mistakes about it, His heavenly host is on assignment to perform His will, and one of the things that involves His will is that of divine and supernatural protection.

Be encouraged, saint!

CHAPTER 4

ANGELS AND HEALING

Angels play an intricate role in God's people receiving healing. Since they aid and assist in bringing the supernatural into the natural, this also includes divine healing whether it is being healed from a sickness or disease plaguing a person's body for years—or a creative miracle or emotional healing.

I've read many accounts of those transported to Heaven, whether by way of divine transportations or death, and God allowing that individual to return to earth to share stories of seeing storehouses in Heaven. And many mentioned seeing storehouses with body parts. Everything a person needs from a natural standpoint can be pulled out of the supernatural realm. The realm where God, Jesus, Holy Spirit, and His holy angels dwell.

Prayer is vital to the believer tapping into the spirit realm, exercising his or her God-given rights and pulling down what is rightfully theirs. *"Your kingdom come. Your will be done on earth as it is in heaven"* (Matthew 6:10). There is no sickness in Heaven.

When you pray, angels respond. Psalm 103:20 (KJV), *"angels…hearkening unto the voice of his word,"* can be interpreted in different ways.

This same piece is found in Chapter 2, but I've included it again in this portion of the book because it is imperative to speak the Word of God over your life when healing is needed.

> *Bless the Lord, ye his angels, that excel in strength, that do his commandments, hearkening unto the voice of his word* (Psalm 103:20 KJV).

As I dissect this Scripture, I want you to understand the magnitude of what you pray and what you speak out of your mouth.

Angels "hearken." Hearken means to:

- Give heed or attention to what is said; listen

- Give respectful attention

- Pay attention

Hearken: a primitive root; to prick up the ears, i.e., hearken: attend, (cause to) hear (-ken), give heed, incline, mark (well), regard. 1) to hear, be attentive, heed, incline (of ears), attend (of ears), hearken, pay attention, listen. Incline, attend (of ears), hearken, pay attention, listen.

Angels hearken to carry out God's plans; and since healing is part of God's will, when you pray healing Scriptures, the angels respond. Angels are focused and adamant about carrying out the will of God. They are adamant about adhering to God's instructions and orders. "Adamant" is defined as refusing to be persuaded or to change one's mind.

ANOINTING

When someone prays under the anointing, when someone prophesies under the anointing, when someone intercedes under the anointing, that person is praying, prophesying, and interceding from a heavenly place. The place where portals are open, where angels are released, ascending and descending, the place where answers are given and granted.

Let's discuss the anointing. Anointing means to smear on or rub on with oil. Another meaning for the word "anointed" is "chosen one." The

Bible says that Jesus Christ was anointed by God with the Holy Spirit to spread the Good News.

In the Greek, the word "anointing" means, according to Strong's Concordance 5545, *chrisma* pronounced khris'-mah from 5548; an unguent or smearing, i.e., (figuratively) the special endowment ("chrism") of the Holy Spirit: anointing, unction.

Angels are attracted to the anointing and they pay attention to the Word of God. When the Word of the God is going forth, they respectfully pay attention, they heed and they listen. They are focused and they execute the plans and the Word of God.

Since prophecy is revealing the mouth of God and revealing the heart of God, let me note this: when prophecy is going forth, angels are attentive and angels are at work. I've heard of many stories of angels showing up while the ministers were preaching, prophesying, teaching, and praying for the people. Angels work with the ministers of the gospel. I've seen them in the pulpit and could feel them granting me the strength to minister. Ministers are identified as a flame of fire in Hebrews: "And of the angels He says: 'Who makes His angels spirits and his ministers a flame of fire'" (Hebrews 1:7).

SPEAK THE WORD AND ACTIVATE YOUR ANGELS

God created the heavens and the earth. Everything that was formed into existence was spoken first by His words. Since we are created in the image of God, this clearly proves how powerful our words are. When we speak the Word of God from heartfelt faith, the Father watches over the words to make it good.

> *Bless the Lord, you His angels, who excel in strength, who do His word, heeding the voice of His word. Bless the Lord all you His hosts, you ministers of His, who do His pleasure* (Psalm 103:20-21).

Are you putting your angels to work? Are you releasing the word by faith? If you could see in the spirit at this very moment, would you see your angels fighting for you, moving on your behalf—or would you see them standing still with tied hands waiting for orders. Yes, it is that serious! The words you speak out of your mouth are so important!

One of the main ways you release and command the host of Heaven is with your words. When you speak the Word of God, the angels hearken unto the voice of your word, but when you speak things contrary to the Word of God, the angels can't carry it out. We know from Scripture that the Holy Spirit can be grieved, but do you also know that you can grieve angels? They are created to listen and respond to the Word of God.

Activate means:

- to make active or more active: such as (1) to make (something, such as a molecule) reactive or more reactive (2) to convert (something, such as a provitamin) into a biologically active derivative; to make (a substance) radioactive

- to set up or formally institute (an organized group, such as a military unit) with the necessary personnel and equipment (2) to put (an individual or unit) on active duty

Active means:

- characterized by action rather than by contemplation or speculation, an *active* life

- producing or involving action or movement; *of a verb form or voice*; asserting that the person or thing represented by the grammatical subject performs the action represented by the verb. *Hits* in "he hits the ball" is *active*.

When we look closer as to what angels do, we see that they minister or serve those who are God's chosen. The Greek word for minister in this passage is *diakonia,* which means to attend, as a servant, aid. His angels guard those who honor the Lord and rescues them from danger.

> *The angel of the Lord encamps all around those who fear Him, and delivers them* (Psalm 34:7).

Reverence means to honor or respect felt or shown; deference; *especially* profound adoring awed respect. Angels reside with those who reverence, a healthy fear of, the Lord. They dwell with those who have a deep respect for the Lord.

Encamp means to settle in or establish a camp, especially a military one. In the Greek, encamp is, according to Strong's Concordance 4637, *skenoo,* pronounced skay-no'-o from 4636; to tent or encamp, i.e., (figuratively) to occupy (as a mansion) or (specially), to reside (as God did in the Tabernacle of old, a symbol of protection and communion): dwell.

ANGEL TESTIMONY
by Apostle Juanita Woodson

(God sent an angel to heal Juanita's newborn baby. This testimony was conducted on my prayer call, interview style.)

And so, we are talking about angels. The Lord had begun to take me back when I was thinking, *Well, what in the world can I share as it relates to angels?* I've had a few different experiences, not a whole lot that I can pinpoint. You would be surprised actually how often we engage with angels. You would be surprised at how many times angels have come in and they have saved you, spared you, stepped in the way of danger, deterred enemies away from you, away from hurt, harm, and danger.

You would be surprised just how many times we have encountered angels. This particular situation was when I was in the hospital and I had just given birth to my daughter. She had been prophesied over before she was born that she would be a prophet and that there was something very special about her. During this particular time, I was not sold out to the Lord. I had not given God a full yes, believe it or not. I was running. I wanted to do my own thing. I decided I was going to put it on hold. I was going to put my calling on hold, going to put my anointing on hold. I was a pastor's kid who was hurt and was running. I was sick of church at that particular point. You may understand how that is.

I was nine months along in the pregnancy and the doctor said it was time to go ahead and have the baby. I was in a lot of pain and I was very big so the doctor induced me. The baby arrives and it was an awesome delivery, everything was great. I had her in about four hours. She was so cute, she looked like me but she was really tiny, very small. She weighed a little over five pounds. That was a little odd because we all thought she was going to be bigger. Then we noticed something was wrong. She started turning grey. The nurses came in and said, "Ma'am, we want to make sure that she's breathing okay." Her heart rate started to change for the worse. She wasn't breathing properly, so they started monitoring her and then said, "We're going to put a little oxygen mask on her and this should do it. Her lungs were probably still developing." They also thought there may have been a little bit of fluid that needed to come out. So they suctioned her lungs to make sure they were clear.

They put the mask on her and I noticed they kept coming in every so often; every hour they would turn the machine up a little bit. At this point, I was thinking, *Okay, something is going on here. Lord, I don't play with my kids. I can't have any problems, no issues. I have never had anything like this before.* Doctors and nurses kept coming in. They turned the machine up a little more and then a little more.

Then I was told, "We're going to put little tubes up her nose. Maybe she's not able to breathe in the mist that's coming from the little mask. We'll put little tubes up the nostrils and see if that can help her breathe." So, of course, babies don't like that, so she's messing with it a little bit.

Finally the doctor came in and said, "We're going to have to actually put her on a breathing machine. We're going to have to sedate her." At this point, I'm thinking, Lord Jesus, what in the world is going on?

I was told, "We're going to put her in the ICU. We don't understanding why she's not breathing yet and we're going to have to do some other things." They started putting tubes into my baby. As you can imagine, I'm about to lose it at this point because they're telling me all the different tubes they have to use—one so she can breathe, one so she can eat and one to keep her sedated.

I asked, "Sedated?"

"Yes ma'am. We're going to put her in a coma state so that she won't be discomforted and she won't be gagging and trying to fight what we need to do to help her. We want her to relax and be calm. It's going to be okay."

No, they didn't tell me that. They're not allowed to tell you that. They said, "We do this all the time. We're just trying to help her to get ready to breathe on her own. You can't take her home."

At this point, we've been in the hospital about three days and was told, "We have to send you home because the time that is allotted for you to be here with your baby has passed. You can't stay here."

So, can you imagine how I felt when I see all these tubes and cords in my baby and she's hooked up to machines? She's in an incubator. I can't hold her. I can't comfort her. I can't breastfeed her. My breasts are overloaded with milk. There was nothing I could do. I wanted to bond with her and I want to be with her. She looked like me, my little twin. And then they send me home. Here I am, detached from my child. Maybe you can attest to that feeling. When you have a baby, there's an attachment you can't even explain. And so, I'm just a wreck.

Lord, what is going on?

My father, a pastor, visited me. He comes in and gives me this look like *I think God is trying to get your attention.* I had seen this look many times before. I had been running away from ministry for a long time. I'd run away from getting my stuff together to do God's will or even just to serve Him and be saved, because I was churched out. I was sick and tired of going to church every day. I mean it was always something.

The Lord began to use my father to tell me that it was time for me to give God a real *yes.* He said what you need to do is go on a three-day fast. You need to repent, you need to ask the Lord to forgive you, and you need to give Him a real yes. He said God is not going to turn this thing around until you give Him a yes.

And so, I listened to my father. I acquiesced to him and I decided, *All right, this is what I'm going to do.* Lord, I'm going to go on this fast because I believe that when I give You a yes and put my will down and pick up Your will, You can work this out. I said, "God, if this is what You want, this is what I want, because You know I love my baby." And so, I began to fast. The Lord began to purify me. I went on a three-day whole fast, no water, no nothing. I wanted nothing but God. I stayed in the presence of God.

I received calls from the hospital giving me updates about my baby. I was there all day and then would go home in the evenings. I was praying. I was praying over her. I was committing myself to God. I was telling him, "Lord, I'm sorry. You know what I've been through. You know what I'm going through, but give it all up to You. I trust You." I began to deal with me and tell the Lord that I was ready to submit.

Sometimes the Lord will use circumstances and situations in your life to help you say yes. People don't believe God would allow you to go through affliction just so He can get that yes up out of you—but the Lord can and He will and He has. My baby was in the hospital and there was no change in her condition after about day four. Day five, there was no change. Day six, there was no change. As a matter of fact, they had maxed out everything they could do for her.

My baby was healed!

On day seven, the phone rang and I was told, "We need you to come to the hospital." As you can imagine, my heart was boom, boom, booming in my chest. *Oh my God, what are they going to tell me, Jesus? No, I'm going to believe. I won't be intimidated by this.* When I arrived at the hospital, the doctor came out to meet me. She said, "I don't know what in the world happened, but your baby pulled out her tubes last night. The one that was way down in her lung was lying beside her…she's been breathing on her own all night."

The Holy Spirit began to talk to me. He said an angel went into my baby's room and took the tube out. *What?* I had never known anything about angels. I had never heard any experiences about people and angels. I come from a very traditional background, a place where something like that is mystical, talking about angels and angels coming to help you. It could be seen as something that's reserved only for the higher-ups in churches or maybe as a pastor. But the Lord said an angel of the Lord visited my baby that night. Hallelujah! Hallelujah!

The doctor said, "There is no way that this child, being sedated, could have pulled the tube out." No one knew what happened. I said, "I know exactly what happened. I gave God a real YES. I told God that I would do what He called me to do. Because of that, He sent the angel of the Lord to come and deliver my child. Hallelujah! God had come and He had visited her!"

I knew that the Lord had sent the answer. I knew that it was nobody but God. They pulled every tube and cord out of her and unhooked her from all those machines. My baby woke up and she was 100 percent healthy—nothing was wrong with her. Hallelujah! Praise God!

Fasting can get your spirit in such a place where you can believe God, you will begin to trust God. I began to go into a trance during those fasting days. I couldn't even remember what the nurses were saying to me until after my baby recovered and the Lord brought what happened during that time. While I was with my baby at the hospital during the days when I was fasting, the nurses had said, "Mother, are you okay to be in here with the healthy babies? Are you okay knowing that your baby may die?" They didn't necessarily say those words, but the Lord had blocked all of that out because it would have caused me to doubt and caused me to fear. Those things would have caused me to want to throw in the towel or be saddened and get my eyes off God.

When you get ready to put your eyes on the Lord and do exactly what He has called you to do, when you're ready to really submit to the will of God in your life, and when you tell God yes and really mean it, God will give you supernatural strength, supernatural faith, supernatural hope.

So because that is the decision I made, the angels of the Lord were called to the scene. My God, the angels of God came to see about my faith. They came to see about my trust in God. They came to answer prayers because I was giving God a real yes.

Don't you know the angels of God are watching? They are looking to see who will really give God a yes, who really want to do God's will, who will be all sold out, who will fast and pray until they get a breakthrough. Just like Daniel, he fasted and prayed for an answer and Michael the archangel came. Even though he was held up for a season, even though the prince of Persia, the demonic realm, was fighting against him, Daniel turned to seek God to get an answer. The Lord sent the breakthrough. Hallelujah!

So it is not ironic to me that the woman of God, Lenika, has written a book about fasting, how God has broken chains and He has called her to be an increase of faith, called her to be prosperous, and called the angels of God to be loosed on her behalf—because that's when they come. They come to see about the Word of God. They come to hear and help those who are obedient, and those who have been sold out and giving God a yes.

I pray this testimony from Juanita has been a blessing to you.

SPEAK THE WORD

If you are in need of healing, speak the Word! Speak healing Scriptures over your life. Decree and declare the Word of the Lord. Angels hearken to the Word of God. No matter how things look, always believe God at His Word. Seek the Lord for answers and He will bring answers. Also, remember that God brings healing in different ways.

The following are examples in Scripture of our Lord releasing healing to His people in different ways. If we aren't careful about being in tune and yielded to the Lord, we can miss our healing. At times, there is also a teaching happening behind the scenes, and if we aren't in tune or sensitive to the Spirit, we cannot only miss the lesson for ourselves but we can also miss it for those who are attached to us.

HEALING SCRIPTURES

Worship the Lord your God, and his blessing will be on your food and water. I will take away sickness from among you (Exodus 23:25 NIV).

If my people, who are called by my name, will humble themselves and pray and seek my face and turn from their wicked ways, then I will hear from heaven, and will forgive their sin and heal their land (2 Chronicles 7:14 NIV).

The Lord nurses them when they are sick and restores them to health (Psalm 41:3 NLT).

He sent His word and healed them, and delivered them from their destruction (Psalm 107:20).

…You restore my health and allow me to live! (Isaiah 38:16 NLT)

But he [Jesus] *was pierced for our transgressions, he was crushed for our iniquities; the punishment that brought us peace was on him, and by his wounds we are healed* (Isaiah 53:5 NIV).

Then your light will break forth like the dawn, and your healing will quickly appear; then your righteousness will go before you, and the glory of the Lord will be your rear guard (Isaiah 58:8 NIV).

Heal me, O Lord, and I shall be healed; save me, and I shall be saved, for You are my praise (Jeremiah 17:14).

"For I will restore health to you and heal you of your wounds," says the Lord… (Jeremiah 30:17).

Behold, I will bring it health and healing; I will heal them and reveal to them the abundance of peace and truth (Jeremiah 33:6).

Is anyone among you sick? Let them call the elders of the church to pray over them and anoint them with oil in the name of the Lord. And the prayer offered in faith will make the sick person well; the Lord will raise them up... (James 5:14-15 NIV).

MY UNCLE SAW JESUS HEALING HIM

This testimony is about my uncle, my mother's brother, who had a brain injury that he sustained when someone attacked him. All we know is that they beat him, they hit him in the head several times, and they left him for dead. When we received the phone call, he was in the hospital. The outcome didn't sound good; the doctors were saying if he did live, he would probably be in a persistent vegetative state (PVS). I decided to share with you how God raised up my uncle on the thirty-third day.

My uncle was in the hospital's intensive care unit in a coma. His wife was a praying woman who stayed by his side. She is not the Holy Ghost, fire-baptized, tongue-talking woman whom we hear about praying the house down; and I share this because as believers we have to understand how *powerful* the *Word of God* is! And how powerful our prayers are when they are pure. No matter how new our walk is with the Lord, as we pray His Word, things change—and change they did for my uncle!

During the time his wife was in the hospital with him, she pulled out the Word of the Lord. She sat there with her Bible, quoting Isaiah 53:5, "He was wounded for our transgressions, He was bruised for our iniquities; the chastisement for our peace was upon Him, and by His stripes, we are healed." She kept quoting that Word over and over again and speaking the Word of the Lord in his room.

During this time I remember having a dream; and in this dream I saw Uncle Junie being raised up from the dead. My husband and I and my sister-in-love Dawn and brother-in-love Matthew drove to Washington, DC, to visit my uncle when he was in the hospital.

When we went to see my uncle in DC, the only anointing I felt on me was the anointing that affects my knees. My knees were burning badly, which means submission. My thoughts were, *How in the world does a dead man submit? There's a dead man lying there.* He wasn't moving, wasn't talking, just lying there with life gone out of him. But I wondered, *How in the world can a dead man submit?* But what the Lord was actually saying to me was, "Submit to the will of God that is on your life." The Lord wanted my uncle to submit to the will of God that was on his life, submit to the process because God would use this for His glory.

Meanwhile, the family had been going back and forth visiting him, traveling in and out of town to visit him and praying. He laid in that bed for days not responding to anything. On the thirty-third day, he was raised up again and I will never forget what the doctor said. The doctor looked at his wife and said, "I don't know what God you serve, but your God just performed a miracle."

She said, "I serve the God of Abraham, Isaac, and Jacob." I remember feeling that my uncle had seen Heaven. I knew it by the Spirit of the Lord that he went to Heaven. But even though I hadn't talked to him yet, I knew that he had been to the other side. I had a stirring feeling that was so overwhelming.

I called him and said, "Uncle Junie, I know you've seen something. Tell me about your experience." He said he saw the Lord Jesus Christ. God did not allow him to see His face, but he literally saw the Lord Jesus Christ. My uncle told me that Jesus was clothed in a silver robe and was rubbing His head. This was so profound because the Lord called my uncle by his nickname. My uncle is named after my grandfather, James MacMillan, but my uncle's nickname is Junie, and ever since he was a child everyone called him Junie. That was the name the Lord called him.

My uncle also shared with me that he saw the Lord Jesus Christ sitting in a tall chair and He was rubbing His head when He called him by his nickname. Uncle Junie said he also saw some other familiar faces in Heaven, which is a beautiful place.

A few months after everything occured, I went home to Virginia to surprise my mom for her birthday. Uncle Junie and his wife were there as well and he talked about when he was in the coma. He said when he went to the other side, off to the left it was dark and dreary but when he turned the other way, there was bright white light and he saw robes and what seemed like billions of people. He shared that the Lord rubbed his (my uncle's) head three times and the fourth time he was healed. Uncle Junie said he asked the Lord, "Am I going to be okay?" Jesus said, "If I tell you that you are going to be all right, you are going to be all right!" This was a beautiful miracle!

I share that story because if you are dealing with a loved one who may be sick or even on his or her "deathbed," don't lose hope and don't give up because healing happened to my uncle and it can happen to someone else.

Uncle Junie was a walking miracle. He has since then transitioned on home to be with the Lord, but I want to note that God gave him fifteen more years on this earth, just as He did Hezekiah after he was healed from being brain dead (2 Kings 20:5-6).

HEALING MIRACLE OF A LITTLE GIRL

One day I received a text saying, "PRAY! My niece has been hit by a car!" That was all, no other information. I went into prayer mode but also panic mode trying to find out if my business partner's niece was still alive. It turns out that she had received a phone call from her sister who was hysterically crying, rightfully so, that her young daughter ran into the street and was hit by a car. They were on their way to the hospital to find out how the girl was doing.

I started sending text messages to my prayer warrior sisters and friends. My stance became very strong and I knew this was war. *Not on my watch,* as I thought about this being one of my very own children. *If this was my baby, I would want strong prayer warriors interceding and calling on the name of the Lord over her life.* I instructed them to *speak life* over this child. I sent a picture of the little girl and started declaring the Word of the Lord and asked them to do the same. *"I will not die, but live, and tell of the works of the Lord"* (Psalm 118:17 NASB).

The next morning as I was in my bathroom getting ready for the day, a strong burden came upon me and the Spirit began to show me very clearly that a spirit of death was sent to this family to attack this child. As I stood there in my bathroom, I felt war in the heavenlies. I felt wickedness in high places. The Holy Spirit began to give me specific instructions and one was to call a prayer-line group of selected prayer warriors, prophets, intercessors, and ministers to come together and pray on behalf of this child.

I orchestrated the prayer assignment and that night we went in praying and covering this baby one after one, also relying on the Spirit of God to lead us as we were going into battle. We were on the phone for almost two hours interceding over this precious child. God began to speak concerning this young girl and said what a miracle and testimony she would be. The doctors told her mother that there was a chance she would not walk again and spoke other tragic things contrary to what she has overcome today. Although she remained in the hospital for some time, her recovery was far quicker than expected and she has been able to defy the odds of what the doctors predicted. (To protect the child's privacy, names were not cited regarding this miracle testimony.)

Intercessors and ministers, we must always be alert—waiting and willing to stand in the gap when the alarm sounds. That day the alarm went off and I wholeheartedly believe because of intercession, the outcome was very different.

SWEET FRAGRANCE IN MY PRAYER ROOM

Thirty minutes prior to praying, I was very weak and tired. In fact, I was battling with illness myself during this time. As I lay in my prayer room on the couch preparing my spirit for the war zone we were about to enter into, a sweet smell entered the room. The aroma was out of this world, *literally.* I began to feel angels all around me as they entered to make the path clear so our prayers would not only be heard, but our prayers would be heeded. I was so pleased that God allowed me to smell this scent and it perked up my spirit, even though I was very tired and in pain.

I also believe God allowed the angels to fill my prayer room with a sweet presence to thank me for being obedient to the call. Saints, your obedience is not contingent upon your feelings and your emotions. When there is a life at stake, we do what we have to do for the sake of the call. This fragrance was so soft, a different smell from anything else. I've smelled the heavenly roses at times, but this was very different—one of the most beautiful fragrances I've experienced in my life. I also saw a yellow-gold color being released into the atmosphere. In my heart, it represented a healing anointing.

TESTIMONY

by Tammie Walker Smith

(This testimony is about how closing legal doors in the spirit relates to healing *not* being received. We have to give the Lord and His holy angels something to work with. Have you ever heard of individuals *not* being healed due to unforgiveness? The following story is not particularly about unforgiveness, but there is a strong connection to repentance and healing. May this story bless you.)

In 1990, I had severe abdominal pain. I went to the doctor and was told that I had some small cysts and fibrosis. I was scheduled for surgery and they removed what they could. I began to feel so much better, but in 2004 the pain returned. For months I took pain medication to ease the pain, but it got worse and the pain medication didn't work anymore. I went to the doctor and he said the cysts and fibrosis were growing back rapidly. Some were the size of eggs and apples and one was the size of a small cantaloupe. The doctor said I needed a hysterectomy.

I was scheduled for surgery February 5, 2005. I got a phone call from my uncle saying, "Tammie, I think you need to pray and repent and ask the Lord to heal your body." Yes, I believe in prayer and yes, I have prayed and prayed for the Lord to heal my body—but I didn't want to pray anymore because I knew God had already heard my prayers. I went to bed thinking about what my uncle said, but I refused to make my body get out of bed to pray that night. I was so bitter and stubborn; I was not mad at God, but I was disappointed because I knew I would never have children.

I laid in bed a little longer, then I put one leg on the floor. Refusing to get on my knees to pray, I got up and went over to the stairs, sat down on a step, and looked out the window. I began to pray and told the Lord, "I know You heard me praying, but I'm still in so much pain." I begin to cry like a baby and then I heard some crazy instructions from the Holy Spirit, "Stand on one leg, Tammie. Jump up and down, Tammie. Get on the scale, Tammie!"

I thought I was going nuts! But I did what I heard and then felt like a *real* nut! However, I was obedient. I sat back down and began to pray and then I began to repent. I tried to think of everything I ever did that was wrong. When I was in the second grade, I was so bad, so I began to repent for that. When I was in third grade, I stole my teacher's ring. When I was twenty, I destroyed a lady's rose garden. I asked the Lord for forgiveness for everything that I could possibly think of.

When I was done, I told the Lord, "I can't think of anything else, but I know You know what I did that was not pleasing in Your sight, so please forgive me. Lord, I'm truly repenting even of the unknown things that I have forgotten about." I got up off the stairs and went to bed and fell asleep. The next day my uncle took me to the doctor's office for my last ultrasound before my surgery, which was scheduled in a few days. The technician got me situated and began to look at the cysts and fibrosis. She said to raise up a little, and I did. I said to myself with confidence, *I'm healed!*

Yes, I was still in a lot of pain, but my confidence was something that I would not let go of. I didn't care if I was still in pain, I believed I was healed! When the tech went out of the room, I rejoiced like I had made a football touchdown! I left the doctor's office and my uncle took me to lunch. When I returned home, the doctor called me personally and asked, "What have you been doing?"

I said, "What? I don't understand your question." Now remember, I'm still in pain while speaking to him on the phone.

He said, "Your ultrasound showed that some of your cysts and fibroids have disappeared and the majority have shrunk."

I said, "I've been praying and using natural herbs."

He said, "Well, it worked! Tammie, you don't need surgery—there is no need for it. Just rest."

Oh my goodness, I screamed with joy and jumped up and down, still hurting with joy! I thanked the Lord, called my uncle, called my mother and sister crying and screaming! "I don't have to have a hysterectomy, the doctor said I was fine, there was no need for surgery!" I told my family about God's healing power and His amazing love for me and they were amazed at what the Lord had done in my life. To this day I never had any more pain and I still to this day have my womb! Can somebody scream, "TO GOD BE THE GLORY!"

HEAVENLY ROSE FRAGRANCE

My husband's father had just received word regarding his health. A few days later, and I mean a few days later, things went downhill really fast. As the immediate family went to hear what the doctors' reports were, my husband's mother instructed all of them to spend intimate time with Dad. If I remember correctly, each son and daughter had their night alone with him. The night my husband was at the hospital with his dad, the Lord dealt with me very strongly and told me to share with our two oldest daughters, who were teenagers at the time, that God was calling their granddad home. We had prayed for the healing of his body, but God must have needed him in Heaven to fulfill other plans.

Sometimes we may never understand all that Heaven does until we meet Jesus face to face. As I began to delicately and prophetically share with our two oldest daughters what the Lord impressed upon me to share with them, a beautiful rose scent filled the room. I can't recall if they smelled it or not, and as difficult and painful as this was for me to do, I believed it was God's way of sharing with me that I heard correctly and it was confirmed for me. It was not an easy task to share with my children, who greatly loved their granddaddy, that he was about to transition to Heaven.

The transition took place a few days later. I recall during the transition and time of physical death—spiritual eternal life—I saw the brightest light that I'd ever witnessed before in my life; and although it was very sad, a peace and glory filled the room. Jesus Christ or a holy angel came to transport him to Heaven. A little time had passed and we were in the room awaiting the funeral home to come for Dad's body and I remember seeing gold dust on his hands. Gregg's mom and sisters also saw the gold dust. I once heard that when you die in Christ, shortly afterward the angels will come and prepare the body. These heavenly signs surrounding Dad's transition reminds us and gives us hope that when we lose someone so precious to us that they are precious to Jesus too and they have special experiences as they enter into Heaven.

Sometimes healing doesn't take place on this side of Heaven. We have to understand that our will is also involved in the process. I share this because even with Gregg's father, the family was believing for divine healing to take place. But the night my husband stayed with his father, he had a vision that his dad took off his hospital robe and started running into a beautiful field.

HEALING FOR AN APPOINTED SEASON ACCORDING TO GOD'S WILL

Some trials in our lives happen because the Lord has allowed them, plainly put. In other words, there are certain things the enemy brings and sends—and there are specific God-ordained issues that God has allowed so that His glory can be revealed. I'm not saying that God causes sickness and disease because He can't give you what He doesn't have; however, He can allow healing not to take place at a particular time so that His power may be demonstrated at a later date. Again, fasting will help you determine and have an insight whether you need to fight or rest. Does that make sense? I hope so!

Let us examine two different scenarios in Scripture to gain some understanding. As you will see in John chapter 9, God's healing was for an appointed season and time, as it pertained to the will of the Father. Scripture declares the man was blind from birth so that the glory of God could be revealed through him—at that particular time.

Then we will examine Second Corinthians 12. Paul was dealing with something the Lord didn't answer through prayer. We don't know if it had to do with an illness or sickness. We do know that although God did not remove it, His glory was revealed through Paul's life.

Before proceeding, please read John chapter 9 in its entirety.

Scenario 1

Now as Jesus passed by, He saw a man who was blind from birth. And His disciples asked Him, saying, "Rabbi, who sinned, this man or his parents, that he was born blind?" Jesus answered, "Neither this man nor his parents sinned, but that the works of God should be revealed in him." ...And they asked them, saying, "Is this your son, who you say was born blind? How then does he now see?" (John 9:1-3,19).

It is apparent that generational curses are real. In fact, in this Scripture passage, the disciples wanted to know who sinned, was it one of his parents? Jesus answered, *"Neither this man nor his parents sinned, but that the works of God should be revealed in him."* It is wise for us to seek God to understand the source. Some things may be generational, something may be there so that the power of God may be made manifest, be revealed, in a person's life.

And during those moments when there is an appointed time, we have to rest in the Lord just as Paul did in the following verses. The *only* way to know this for sure is by revelation given to you by God.

Before proceeding, please read Second Corinthians chapter 12 in its entirety.

Scenario 2

For this thing I besought the Lord thrice, that it might depart from me (2 Corinthians 12:8).

It is doubtless not profitable for me to boast. I will come to visions and revelations of the Lord (verse 1). Of such a one I will boast; yet of myself I will not boast, except in my infirmities. For though I might desire to boast, I will not be a fool; for I will speak the truth. But I refrain, lest anyone should think of me above what he sees me to be or hears from me. And lest I should be exalted above measure by the abundance of the revelations, a thorn in the flesh was given to me, a messenger of Satan to buffet me, lest I be exalted above measure. Concerning this thing I pleaded with the Lord three times that it might depart from me. And He said to me, "My grace is sufficient for you, for My strength is made perfect in weakness." Therefore most gladly I will rather boast in my infirmities, that the power of Christ may rest upon me. Therefore I take pleasure in infirmities, in reproaches, in needs, in persecutions, in distresses, for Christ's sake. For when I am weak, then I am strong (verses 5-10). *Did I take advantage of you by any of those whom I sent to you? I urged Titus, and sent our brother with him. Did Titus take advantage of you? Did we not walk in the same spirit? Did we not walk in the same steps? Again, do you think that we excuse ourselves to you? We speak before God in Christ. But we do all things, beloved, for your edification* (verses 17-19). *Lest, when I come again, my God will humble me among you, and I shall mourn for many who have sinned before and have not repented of the uncleanness, fornication, and lewdness which they have practiced* (verse 21).

A few verses have been pulled out of this chapter in Second Corinthians 12 for examination. In this passage of Scripture, we aren't told exactly what Paul was dealing with and going through, but it is obvious that he didn't want to go through it. How do we know that? Because he prayed and sought the Lord three times. It states in the Scripture in verse 8, *"Concerning this thing I pleaded with the Lord three times that it might depart from me."*

Let it be known that this is a clear indication that if Paul had fasted until he was blue in the face, the *"thorn"* would not have been removed. Could it be that this thorn was an intricate part of his ministry assignment so that the *"power of Christ"* could rest upon him?

A thorn is defined as a stiff, sharp-pointed, straight or curved woody projection on the stem or other parts of a plant; a source of discomfort, annoyance, or difficulty; an irritation or an obstacle.

Paul had been taken to Heaven; and although he went through great sufferings for the Lord, he was allowed to experience some beautiful things in God as well. The Lord had to keep him in a place of humility—hence, the thorn in his flesh. That is what happens in many instances when God has a strong mantle on a person's life. Many sufferings are expected and great trials are presented. So, there is a need to seek after God constantly as we goes through life. As God begins to elevate us, if we begin to walk in pride, it can become very dangerous. Afflictions are presented, or allowed, so there is indeed a common ground for humility.

Whatever you may be dealing with, it is imperative you get revelation from God about it. I've also discovered that God can change His mind. You may be going through something similar to Paul so that the glory of Christ will rest strongly on you. I still encourage you to petition the throne, presenting your case before the Father, the Judge, just as He changed His mind and gave Hezekiah fifteen more years, He may do the same for you. Regardless how things unfold, God will give you the grace and strength to endure!

WE SPOKE THE WORD AND OUR DAUGHTER WAS HEALED

This is a story about my baby named Joy. As I write, I'm thinking back to when I watched my baby stand as the school officials announced her name; tears filled my eyes as well as my heart. During the course of 6th through 8th grade, Joy made straight A's on her report card and was accepted into college early. She will actually be graduating from high school with a college Associate's degree.

Allow me to go back about twelve years. My little Joy was such a sweet and special child, but I started to notice some delay in her speech and communication skills. I based this delay on the growth of my other daughters.

I took Joy to the doctor and I asked for an assessment. She agreed and an assessment was done for the age range of eighteen to twenty-two months. It was discovered that she was a tad bit behind in her development and her learning. My husband and I did not receive this news.

Instead, my husband and I spoke life! We spoke life over her by constantly telling our baby that she was intelligent, she was smart, and she could do anything. As we have seen things unfold for her throughout her schoolings, we see how the hand of God responded to our words of life.

I decided to include this in the book because many times we think things are always about a physical healing in terms of a sickness or disease, but this to me was like a reconstruction-of-the-brain type of healing.

AGREEMENT IS POWER!

To me the importance of agreement in prayer is underutilized in the church. I believe we believers, as ministers of the gospel, don't agree enough. Let us all be reminded of the Word concerning healing and the power of agreement. James 5:14-16 (NLT) tells us specifically to come together and God will perform healing miracles:

> *Are any of you sick? You should call for the elders of the church to come and pray over you, anointing you with oil in the name of the Lord. Such a prayer offered in faith will heal the sick, and the Lord will make you well. And if you have committed any sins, you will be forgiven. Confess your sins to each other and pray for each other so that you may be healed. The earnest prayer of a righteous person has great power and produces wonderful results.*

HEALING STORIES IN THE BIBLE

I encourage you to read these and other healing stories in the Bible to build your faith. Don't limit God or place Him in a box—you may never know how healing will come. He may surprise you! I've included a few unusual stories:

- Naaman was healed: read Second Kings 5:9-14.
- Jesus spit on his eyes: read Mark 8:22-25.

• Someone else's faith healed him: read Luke 5:17-26.

As we continue to the next chapter, I encourage you that through whatever comes your way, stay close to God and pray His will for your life and the life of your family.

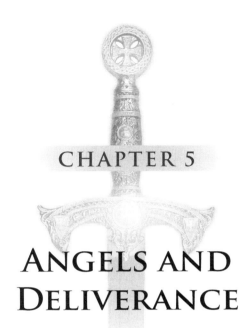

CHAPTER 5

ANGELS AND DELIVERANCE

The name of the Lord is a strong tower; the righteous
run to it and are safe (Proverbs 18:10).

The Word of God has much to say regarding our Father bringing deliverance to His children. As we posture and position ourselves to receive what is rightfully ours, one main point to keep in mind is that His heavenly host and angel army play an extremely large part of Proverbs 18:10 manifesting in our lives.

For it is written, "Thy kingdom come, Thy will be done in earth, as it is in heaven," (Matthew 6:10 KJV). Christ also declares as He taught the disciples to pray, "…**deliver** us from evil: For thine is the kingdom, and the power, and the glory…" (Matthew 6:13 KJV). Deliverance is part of the believer's portion, for it is part of our salvation.

Salvation, which is *soteria* in the Greek, means to rescue, safety, salvation, *deliverance,* and preservation from harm.

When we give our lives to Christ, we inherit angelic assistance for it is our legal right. Salvation allowed us to become *heirs* of God's Kingdom.

Inherit means:

- receive (money, property, or a title) as an heir at the death of the previous holder. "She inherited a fortune from her father."

- become heir to, fall heir to, come into/by, be bequeathed, be left, be willed; be devised. "She inherited her uncle's farm."

- derive (a quality, characteristic, or predisposition) genetically from one's parents or ancestors. "She had inherited the beauty of her grandmother."

- receive or be left with (a situation, object, etc.) from a predecessor or former owner.

Are not all angels ministering spirits sent to serve those who will inherit salvation? (Hebrews 1:14 NIV).

JESUS CHRIST'S PRESENCE BRINGS DELIVERANCE

During the service where Jesus Christ appeared—the story mentioned in Chapter 1—there was such fire and deliverance that fell in the house of the Lord. This was different from other times, in that normally when deliverance hits a church or ministry, believers are laid out, slain on the floor. This time, though, as the cloud of glory and fire of God filled the room, we all just sat in His presence silently, not wanting to leave, not wanting to speak, talk, move, or budge. It was one of those types of services and visitations that you hunger and thirst for, one never to be forgotten.

After we finally left the service, an electric charge went through my body. When I feel the anointing of deliverance, it comes on my right hand. This is what I felt, yet it was so strong. It felt like an electric shock going through my right hand. God gave me the revelation that He was bringing strong deliverance to His children. He was delivering them from deep-rooted pain and trauma.

As we drove home and as this anointing rested on me for some time, I started asking the Lord, *What are you doing, what is this?* The Holy Spirit revealed that He was still delivering. When Jesus and the angels showed up during service, Jesus was sending "lightning bolts" through the people and I sincerely believe those lightning bolts were not only sending great power needed for His people to walk in higher levels of destiny, but also a power that would bring forth great deliverance. God began speaking to my heart and said it was a continual burning and a continual deliverance, as many were still being set free as they drove home and throughout the night. Glory!

BEAUTIFUL, BRONZE-COLORED FEATHER APPEARED

When going through a serious battle one day, I prayed and asked God to have Michael release angels to fight on my behalf, which was on a Tuesday. The following Sunday, my husband and I went to dinner with our oldest daughter Jazmine, along with her friend and his parents. When we returned home, laying on the table was a beautiful, bronze-colored feather and it was so defined. Just from the look of this feather, I could instantly tell it was another level, a high-ranking angel. I looked at our daughter, a seer, and asked her what she saw and she said it came out of a portal. I asked with the assurance that she had seen a vision of some sort because this feather was unlike any of the feathers I had witnessed before. The cut was different, the dimensions and shape were different, the texture was different—everything about it was different. It's almost hard to write about from a natural perspective. That is how heavenly defined this beautiful bronze-golden feather was.

We then went into my prayer room and when I placed the feather on my lap, I instantly felt a holy presence. I felt a holy heat, and again I felt that this feather represented a very high-ranking angel. So much so, I was overcome with the fear of the Lord. I asked Jayla again what she saw and she shared that she saw a large angel wing and in the wing there were gold feathers and smaller bronze feathers as well. The same color bronze that appeared on our table. She also said that when she went to use the restroom, out of the corner of her eye, her peripheral vision, she saw a vision of the angel picking up the feather from the table, carefully looking at it, examining it, and placing it back down. She remembers thinking, *I wonder if the feather will be there when I go back in the living room?* And sure enough, when she returned, it was still on the table.

I knew this was a high-ranking angel sent on assignment, responding to the prayers I prayed a few days prior. God allowed this angel to let me know of his existence and that his presence was there battling on my family's behalf. He busted and broke through the heavenlies for us. He was fighting for us as a result of the prayer I prayed earlier in the week.

God revealed to me that due to the nature of the warfare I was experiencing, there needed to be a higher-ranking angel sent on assignment for the task. I received revelation from one of my prayer sisters that God was giving me a different level of access and authority in the realm of the spirit to commission His holy angels. As we prayed for clarity in regard to this angel, she kept hearing the word "commission."

Commission is defined as the act of committing or entrusting a person, group, etc., with supervisory power or authority; an authoritative order, charge, or direction; authority granted for a particular action or function. God also began to share with me that there was more revelation to come regarding this encounter.

Three days later, while I was on the phone sharing this beautiful experience with my sister, I received the revelation as to why the angel picked the bronze feather up and looked at it. The Lord spoke that the angel was given specific instructions by Michael, the chief angel, and the angel wanted to ensure the instructions were carried out as Michael received his instructions from the Lord. The angel was examining the feather. We started praising the Lord and thanking Him!

I can imagine the instructions: You are to leave her one of your bronze feathers. This will serve as a sign that Heaven has heard her prayers. Due to the nature of the warfare she is experiencing, I want to make sure she knows I sent you.

Heaven is strategic! This blessed my soul and reminded me of the fact that our heavenly Father is so orderly and strategic:

> *God is not a God of disorder but of peace—as in all the congregations of the Lord's people* (1 Corinthians 14:33 NIV).
>
> *Let all things be done decently and in order* (1 Corinthians 14:40).

God rebuked me when I decided to send some feather pictures to one of my prayer sisters. In the message, I sent a picture of some of the white feathers God has allowed me to receive, and I was also going to send a picture of the bronze feather I had received. But I felt an inward witness that I was *not* to send the feather pictures in the same text. I did it anyway and afterward, the Father said they are not to be compared as the latter is a higher-ranking angel, in a different class. I instantly repented! To me, this was also a reminder that our understanding of spiritual things is so limited, and there is always more to learn. Heaven is much more vast than we can ever comprehend. However, I do believe there is so much more God wants us to experience and encounter.

After this experience, I felt a strong holy presence for the next few days. It was as if this angel was assigned to handle some serious business in the heavenlies as it related to my family and me, so it stayed around us, in close proximity, for a few days.

Another observation I noticed a few months after this particular feather appeared was that the color dulled a little bit. When we first received this feather, it was glistening and I could see tiny specks of gold within the bronze. When I first took pictures of it, the specks of gold were showing up strong in the pictures.

Because the Lord told me this was a different category of angels, I decided to place this feather in my Bible. Later when I showed someone the feather, I noticed the color changed a little; it wasn't sparkling as much. Since this was a piece of Heaven released to earth, it reminded me of that fact that we as believers get dull if we are not connected to Heaven. It reminded me of the importance of staying in His presence.

Deliverance is defined as the action of being rescued or set free. According to Strong's Concordance 3444, in Hebrew the word is *yshu-w`ah,* pronounced yesh-oo'-aw, the feminine passive participle of 3467; something saved, i.e., (abstractly) deliverance; hence, aid, victory, prosperity: deliverance, health, help(-ing), salvation, save, saving (health), welfare.

MICHAEL THE ARCHANGEL

This portion focuses on the fast as it pertains to Daniel. We'll look at what happened to him and the victory that was won. Because of the nature of the deliverance that took place, I decided to include this material, which is taken from my book, *Fasting for Breakthrough.*

Angels play a very critical part in the breakthrough and deliverance process. Scripture reveals God used angels to bring the answers and revelation Daniel was seeking. When Daniel chose to fast to gain revelation and understanding of his dream, angels not only fought on his behalf but as he fasted and prayed, angels were released to bring the answers. Daniel experienced answered prayers, and he also experienced a breakthrough in the earth realm.

Also, note how Daniel really poured out his heart before the Lord. As you read this chapter, you will see how his prayer was coming from a place of deep humility, not only for himself but for the people as well.

Let us take a look at Daniel chapter 9.

AN ANGEL APPEARED TO DANIEL

In the first year of Darius the son of Ahasuerus, of the lineage of the Medes, who was made king over the realm of the Chaldeans—in the first year of his reign I, Daniel, understood by the books the number of the years specified by the word of the

Lord through Jeremiah the prophet, that He would accomplish seventy years in the desolations of Jerusalem.

Then I set my face toward the Lord God to make request by prayer and supplications, with fasting, sackcloth, and ashes. And I prayed to the Lord my God, and made confession, and said, "O Lord, great and awesome God, who keeps His covenant and mercy with those who love Him, and with those who keep His commandments, we have sinned and committed iniquity, we have done wickedly and rebelled, even by departing from Your precepts and Your judgments. Neither have we heeded Your servants the prophets, who spoke in Your name to our kings and our princes, to our fathers and all the people of the land. O Lord, righteousness belongs to You, but to us shame of face, as it is this day—to the men of Judah, to the inhabitants of Jerusalem and all Israel, those near and those far off in all the countries to which You have driven them, because of the unfaithfulness which they have committed against You.

"O Lord, to us belongs shame of face, to our kings, our princes, and our fathers, because we have sinned against You. To the Lord our God belong mercy and forgiveness, though we have rebelled against Him. We have not obeyed the voice of the Lord our God, to walk in His laws, which He set before us by His servants the prophets. Yes, all Israel has transgressed Your law, and has departed so as not to obey Your voice; therefore the curse and the oath written in the Law of Moses the servant of God have been poured out on us, because we have sinned against Him. And He has confirmed His words, which He spoke against us and against our judges who judged us, by bringing upon us a great disaster; for under the whole heaven such has never been done as what has been done to Jerusalem.

"As it is written in the Law of Moses, all this disaster has come upon us; yet we have not made our prayer before the Lord our

God, that we might turn from our iniquities and understand Your truth" (Daniel 9:1-13).

Continue reading Daniel chapter 9

Did you notice in that prayer how Daniel poured his heart out to God? If you didn't notice, go back and reread the passage. He cried out, he confessed, and he even repented on behalf of others. He really cried out from the heart—and prayers that are prayed from the heart always get Heaven's attention.

> *And suddenly, one having the likeness of the sons of men touched my lips; then I opened my mouth and spoke, saying to him who stood before me, "My lord, because of the vision my sorrows have overwhelmed me, and I have retained no strength. For how can this servant of my lord talk with you, my lord? As for me, no strength remains in me now, nor is any breath left in me." Then again, the one having the likeness of a man touched me and strengthened me. And he said, "O man greatly beloved, fear not! Peace be to you; be strong, yes, be strong!" So when he spoke to me I was strengthened, and said, "Let my lord speak, for you have strengthened me." Then he said, "Do you know why I have come to you? And now I must return to fight with the prince of Persia; and when I have gone forth, indeed the prince of Greece will come. But I will tell you what is noted in the Scripture of Truth. (No one upholds me against these, except Michael your prince)* (Daniel 10:16-21).

Could it be that Michael, one of the highest-ranking angels, was the only one who also had the revelation and understanding of what was going to be released to Daniel? *That is profound!* Imagine why the warfare was so great. Daniel had set out to understand the dream-vision God had given him, but was not able to understand it until an angel of the Lord appeared to him. What this instantly taught me was that even when God gives a dream or a vision to an individual revelation of the dream or vision is not always granted. Though a dream may come, the revelation of the dream may not be released.

At times, it will also take fasting and prayer to release the revelation from Heaven. It is clear that although Daniel had been given the dream-vision, the revelation of the dream had not yet been given, and I repeatedly bring this up because I want to make a point. Many believers misinterpret a dream or a vision, or they share it before it's time and come to their own conclusion before the proper revelation concerning the dream or vision is released. This also serves as a word of wisdom and a word of warning. After the Lord has given you a dream or vision, pray and wait for the interpretation!

Due to the nature and magnitude of Daniel's dream-vision, there was a fight for the knowledge to be released from Heaven. And due to the weight of the information that was to be shared, it was a serious battle in the second heaven. It was so serious that Michael, an archangel, had to come and assist with this battle! It was won but only because of Daniel's persistent assignment and commitment to fasting and prayer!

In the Kingdom of Heaven, things are set up through rankings, hierarchies, and chains of command. Just as it is in the natural on the battleground, if a warrior is not as trained or equipped for battle, another warrior who is better qualified, trained, and equipped will step in and fight so that the battle may be won.

This also reveals why some of our prayers are not answered. You see, the moment Daniel set his face to make prayer to the Lord, his supplication was heard. Notice "heard" not "answered." Hearing and answering are two totally different things.

The angel said, "From the first day," not the second day or the third day, but "**from the first day** that you set your heart to understand, and to humble yourself before God, **your words were heard**…" (Daniel 10:12). Also, notice that the angel did not say Daniel's words were heard and then the Lord answered.

In the King James version of the Bible, instead of the word "humble" it cites the word "chasten," which means to inflict suffering upon for purposes of moral improvement; chastise; to restrain; subdue: to make chaste in style. Yes! Fasting is inflicting oneself, and it was apparent that Daniel did just that for divine purposes.

What is also wonderful is the fact that our Holy God responds when we discipline ourselves for His glory, purposes, and assignment. The problem in many cases is that we don't persevere in fasting and praying long enough so that the time is released through the third heaven to the second heavens, to the earth to manifest. Sometimes we want things as soon as we pray; we do not understand the proper timing and also misunderstand the war that has to be won in the spirit realm so that the manifestation of what we have been praying for is released!

Please don't get me wrong, sometimes there is an instant answer to prayer, and guess what? During those sovereign times when God chooses to move quickly, it is not always understandable. On the contrary, some people remain under an open heaven due to a fasting and praying lifestyle, so when they pray it often seems as if answers are granted with no time awaited. This is because the heavens are already open over them and things generally manifest with ease.

This isn't at all to diminish Daniel's prayer but rather to explain that there is so much more that happens in the spirit realm—far greater than our own earthly understanding. But I sincerely believe that *if* we pray and fast more, and also persevere and wait for the answers, solutions, problems to be solved, and breakthroughs—we will receive answers on a more consistent basis.

FASTING ACTIVATES ANGELIC ACTIVITY

It is very evident based upon the Scripture that much angelic activity was taking place while God was releasing these holy visions to Daniel during his time of fasting and afterward. It is such a beautiful thing that our sacrifice, obedience, seeking, and searching can release God's messengers in our lives. Be mindful of the fact that when you fast and pray, angels are released from Heaven to work on your behalf. Even if you do not see them working behind the scenes, you have to rest in the assurance that God's word is true; and if they showed up for Daniel, they will also show up for you!

Also, note in verse 18 that there was another angel that came to strengthen Daniel:

> *Then again, the one having the likeness of a man touched me and strengthened me. And he said, "O man greatly beloved, fear not! Peace be to you; be strong, yes, be strong!" So when he spoke to me I was strengthened, and said, "Let my lord speak, for you have strengthened me." Then he said, "Do you know why I have come to you? And now I must return to fight with the prince of Persia; and when I have gone forth, indeed the prince of Greece will come. But I will tell you what is noted in the Scripture of Truth. (No one upholds me against these, except Michael your prince.)" ...And he informed me, and talked with me, and said, "O Daniel, I have now come forth to give you skill to understand"* (Daniel 10:18-21; 9:22).

DANIEL RECAP

- Daniel fasted to gain revelation and understanding of a vision.

- He fasted and he prayed.

- Angels were released on Daniel's behalf to bring the answer.

- Daniel experienced answered prayers.

A lot of in-between things happened, but we can see clearly that the breakthrough Daniel needed came to pass as a result of angelic and divine intervention. Glory to God!

AN ANGEL DELIVERED PETER FROM PRISON

Herod the King was so upset he murdered James, John's brother, and he had Peter arrested. All of this happened during the week of Passover, a time when there were many people in Jerusalem. Herod had sixteen soldiers assigned to guard Peter day and night. During the night, Peter was bound to two soldiers by chains. Believers went before the Lord and prayers were sent up for Peter's release. An angel appeared and gave Peter specific instructions; and after Peter obeyed, the chains fell off. Scripture reveals that Peter didn't realize he was actually seeing an angel, he thought he was seeing a vision; nevertheless, he continued to follow the angel. As they passed the guards, they came to a gate and the gate opened by itself.

This is such a beautiful and remarkably detailed story of deliverance. What I glean from this story is that Peter followed instructions and obeyed in a spirit of understanding the totality of what was taking place. He didn't ask questions. As you will see when reading the Scripture passage, the angel said, "Quickly," which was a sure indication that things in the supernatural realm had been properly planned according to the will of God and there was no time to procrastinate, delay, or ask questions.

There are many times when God wants to show forth His glory through deliverance, but we pause and ask questions or we get in the way. I encourage you to keep this story before you in the wake of your deliverance, for you may never know when it will take place.

It was about this time that King Herod arrested some who belonged to the church, intending to persecute them. He had James, the brother of John, put to death with the sword. When he saw that this met with approval among the Jews, he proceeded to seize Peter also. This happened during the Festival of Unleavened Bread. After arresting him, he put him in prison, handing him over to be guarded by four squads of four soldiers each. Herod intended to bring him out for public trial after the Passover.

So Peter was kept in prison, but the church was earnestly praying to God for him.

The night before Herod was to bring him to trial, Peter was sleeping between two soldiers, bound with two chains, and sentries stood guard at the entrance. Suddenly an angel of the Lord appeared and a light shone in the cell. He struck Peter on the side and woke him up. "Quick, get up!" he said, and the chains fell off Peter's wrists.

Then the angel said to him, "Put on your clothes and sandals." And Peter did so. "Wrap your cloak around you and follow me," the angel told him. Peter followed him out of the prison, but he had no idea that what the angel was doing was really happening; he thought he was seeing a vision. They passed the first and second guards and came to the iron gate leading to the city. It opened for them by itself, and they went through it. When they had walked the length of one street, suddenly the angel left him.

Then Peter came to himself and said, "Now I know without a doubt that the Lord has sent his angel and rescued me from Herod's clutches and from everything the Jewish people were hoping would happen."

When this had dawned on him, he went to the house of Mary the mother of John, also called Mark, where many people had gathered and were praying. Peter knocked at the outer entrance, and a servant named Rhoda came to answer the door. When she recognized Peter's voice, she was so overjoyed she ran back without opening it and exclaimed, "Peter is at the door!"

"You're out of your mind," they told her. When she kept insisting that it was so, they said, "It must be his angel."

But Peter kept on knocking, and when they opened the door and saw him, they were astonished. Peter motioned with his hand for them to be quiet and described how the Lord had brought him out of prison. "Tell James and the other brothers and sisters about this," he said, and then he left for another place (Acts 12:1-17 NIV).

ANGEL TESTIMONY
by Prophetess Nadia Sanguinetti-Plunkett

Blessings, it is so encouraging to know God has special agents on assignment just for us. Here is my testimony of angelic presence and visitation:

I've heard so many stories of people experiencing angelic visitation or even the evidence of them being around. From gold dust and flakes, angel feathers, tiny diamond-like gems to oil appearing in unusual places such as books, walls, and ceilings. Some have even physically seen angels in their midst.

The deeper I went in my walk with Christ and learned about the Kingdom of God, even understanding more about the realm of the prophetic as a prophet, I desired to have angelic encounters and experiences. I wanted to know more about these heavenly beings that were doing so much on my behalf. I considered these experiences as God revealing another dimension of His glory. I wanted as much of God's glory to be revealed in my life as I could handle.

One day I was searching Amazon for books on the prophetic and a book popped up as a suggestion titled, *Putting Your Angels to Work* by Norvel Hayes; I immediately ordered it. Once it arrived, I dived right in and started reading this short but powerful book. It was hard to put it down. A few days later, I took my kids to the park to enjoy the gorgeous day. It was warm outside and the skies were pure blue and bright, not a cloud in sight; it was unusually clear. I sat reading the book while the kids were off having fun. I found myself staring at the skies, just marveling at how clear it was; it was such a peaceful feeling.

I received a call from a good friend and sister in Christ asking me to pray for her sister and stand in agreement with her for healing and breakthrough in her life. Right there in the park, I started praying out loud with fervency for her sister; and as we touched and agreed in prayer, I looked up to the sky and behold there was the image of an angel in the cloud. Mind you the sky was still clear, bright and blue, not a cloud in sight except for the image of the angel. It was the most beautiful thing I had ever seen.

I told my friend about it; we were so amazed. I felt such a sense of peace and God's glory at that moment, it was incredible. Then I looked up and there was another angel in the sky; by this time I had to sit down because the glory of God was so overwhelming. We thanked God for the breakthrough prayers and for the angelic visitation. I took a few pictures to capture the moment because I still couldn't believe what I had seen. I was so grateful.

Later in the day, I stopped to pick up some groceries before heading home. I remember saying to the Lord, *I just want my life to be pleasing to You and to make You smile.* When I got to the parking lot of the store, I got out of my car and by now the sky above was filled with soft, rippled clouds, but there was a visible cut through the clouds that resembled a smile. It made my heart melt and smile to see God's smile.

ANGEL TESTIMONY

by Tymesia Butcher

My husband, Tony, was preaching and the anointing of God was resting heavily upon him. As he stepped out from behind the pulpit and began ministering at the altar, an angel hovered over him! It didn't move, it just hovered.

During prayer one night, and other times as well, I began to see snakes falling to the ground and simultaneously, I could see the angels of God flying through the sanctuary. Deliverance was in the house!

There was a time when I was really becoming discouraged in the midst of an assignment that God had given me—a play, *My Redeemer Lives.* I was about to call it quits because things weren't going as planned. On this particular night while we were rehearsing the play, I could see something beneath the seat where Tony and I sit during service. I thought it was trash and decided to get it later.

When rehearsal was over, I went to retrieve whatever was beneath the seat—and I found angel feathers. When we came back to rehearsal two nights later, I found feathers in the pulpit, which made me search around the sanctuary more closely, but I didn't find any more. When we returned for Sunday morning service, I found more feathers that were in a very visible area—where I had searched previously but found nothing. And I found more in the pulpit!

This past Sunday during service while Tony was ministering at the altar, a woman of God for whom he was praying had angel feathers on her. As I was sharing this with my daughter, she said that while Tony was praising God from the pulpit, she could see angel feathers falling off of him!

FINANCES

In addition to healing, one of the most common prayer requests is that of financial blessing and breakthrough. As you meditate and release the following Scriptures over your life, believe God for the impossible. Believe God to release and dispatch His holy angels to bring in your harvest. You may have already sown such seeds into your heavenly account—it is time to receive the rewards!

During these last days, angels will be sent on assignment to release inventions, ideas that will make God's people fortunes, divine strategies, and the like! Get ready, take your position, and step out in faith. I encourage you to study and meditate on these Scriptures as well as the prophetic word God gave me regarding wealth transfer. Be heartened, beloved! God has so much more in store for His children who will walk upright and proclaim their heavenly harvest.

WEALTH SCRIPTURES

1. *The Lord shall increase you more and more, you and your children* (Psalm 115:14 KJV).

2. *The lions may grow weak and hungry, but those who seek the Lord lack no good thing* (Psalm 34:10 NIV).

3. *But you shall remember the Lord your God, for it is He who gives you power to get wealth, that He may establish His covenant which He swore to your fathers, as it is this day* (Deuteronomy 8:18).

4. *The earth is the Lord's, and everything in it, the world, and all who live in it* (Psalm 24:1 NIV).

5. *Beloved, I pray that you may prosper in all things and be in health, just as your soul prospers* (3 John 1:2).

6. *You will be blessed when you come in and blessed when you go out* (Deuteronomy 28:6 NIV).

7. *The blessing of the Lord brings wealth, without painful toil for it* (Proverbs 10:22 NIV).

8. *Humility is the fear of the Lord; its wages are riches and honor and life* (Proverbs 22:4 NIV).

9. *I have been young, and now am old; yet I have not seen the righteous forsaken, nor his descendants begging bread* (Psalm 37:25).

10. *On the first day of every week, each one of you should set aside a sum of money in keeping with your income, saving it up, so that when I come no collections will have to be made* (1 Corinthians 16:2 NIV).

11. *"Bring the whole tithe into the storehouse, that there may be food in my house. Test me in this," says the Lord Almighty, "and see if I will not throw open the floodgates of heaven and pour out so much blessing that there will not be room enough to store it. I will prevent pests from devouring your crops, and the vines in your fields will not drop their fruit before it is ripe," says the Lord Almighty. "Then all the nations will call you blessed, for yours will be a delightful land," says the Lord Almighty* (Malachi 3:10-12 NIV).

12. *A good person leaves an inheritance for their children's children, but a sinner's wealth is stored up for the righteous* (Proverbs 13:22 NIV).

13. *But seek first his kingdom and his righteousness, and all these things will be given to you as well. Therefore do not worry about tomorrow, for tomorrow will worry about itself. Each day has enough trouble of its own* (Matthew 6:33-34 NIV).

14. *The Lord has greatly blessed my master; he has become a wealthy man. The Lord has given him flocks of sheep and goats, herds of cattle, a fortune in silver and gold, and many male and female servants and camels and donkeys* (Genesis 24:35 NLT).

15. *Now Isaac sowed in that land, and reaped in the same year a hundredfold; and the Lord blessed him* (Genesis 26:12).

16. *"Behold, the days are coming," says the Lord, "when the plowman shall overtake the reaper, and the treader of grapes him that sows seed; the mountains shall drip with sweet wine, and all the hills shall flow with it"* (Amos 9:13).

ANGELS, MOSES, AND THE RED SEA

The Angel of God, who went before the camp of Israel, moved and went behind them; and the pillar of cloud went from before them and stood behind them (Exodus 14:19).

God using Moses to part the Red Sea was one of the greatest miracles God performed in the Old Testament. Miracle after miracle God had performed on behalf of His people, finally leading them out of slavery and bondage, away from the brutal hands of the Egyptians. He made a promise which would be fulfilled; He set them free from oppression, captivity, and chains.

When Pharaoh finally let the people go, God didn't lead them on the road that made the most sense. The Bible tells us in Exodus 13 that though the path was shorter right through the Philistine country, God said, "If they face war, they might change their minds and return to Egypt." Rather, God led them around the desert road toward the Red Sea. Hot, dry, barren wasteland. I can almost see the sea looming off in the distance—and hear the grumblings starting and feel the fear rising. As the Israelites got closer, that sea must have looked bigger and deeper. An obstacle that seemed too difficult to overcome. Their eyes were focused on the problem.

I can imagine how many angels were present to help this miracle come to pass. Although Scripture records in Exodus 14:19 that the angel of God, who had been going before the camp of Israel, moved and went behind them. I know beyond a shadow of a doubt that a miracle of this magnitude that affected many souls was performed with *much* angelic activity. God's hosts were present and assisting His people!

> *They ate the food of angels! God gave them all they could hold* (Psalm 78:25 NLT).

> *Then the Lord said to Moses, "I will rain down bread from heaven for you. The people are to go out each day and gather enough for that day. In this way I will test them and see whether they will follow my instructions. On the sixth day they are to prepare what they bring in, and that is to be twice as much as they gather on the other days"* (Exodus 16:4-5 NIV).

TALL ANGEL IN THE PULPIT

I had a similar experience during this particular season in the pulpit of another church where I ministered. I had been laying before the Lord—often in much fasting and prayer and a lot of time laboring—the message that I would deliver to the people of God. When I arrived, I knew beyond any doubt that miracles, signs, healing, and deliverance would fall because of the glorious presence I felt over me.

I even remember the Lord changing the word a day or two before I went to minister. The word of the Lord during that time was repentance and how the people of God needed to turn from their wicked ways and turn back to God. God had given me a word; and as I began to minister, I remember looking to my right, and out of nowhere there was a big, tall angel. This angel stood about twelve to fourteen feet tall. Imagine if you had two tall people standing on top of each other, that is how tall the angel was. I saw it for just a hot second. God allowed me to see the angel for a glimpse, but I believe He sent him there that day on my behalf for the assignment of ministry that would take place.

Angels are real, and what we have to understand and realize is that they are sent by God, and they come to assist God's people in deliverance. They come to aid and help in our ministry to His people. They come to help you in the salvation process, during moments of great breaking when chains are falling off people and bondages are being removed. They come to support the ministers of the Lord—believers carrying out Jesus's commission.

It was very relevant and very apparent on that day that God had sent angels to assist, as there were so many people present to pray for that I could not handle them all. Thankfully, several ministers visited on that day and when the people came to the altar at the end of the service, the other ministers came to assist. One of the ministers looked at one of the girls who always had an anointing on her life and actually saw an angel standing right there. She had the microphone in her hand and told everyone that there was an angel present. Not only did I have a chance to see an angel with my own eyes, there were others in attendance who also experienced the visitation. Angels were there and such deliverance took place.

Always remember, there are more angels for you than people against you! Don't focus on the enemies or the betrayers. Shift your focus to God and His heavenly host, I promise it helps!

The chariots of God are twenty thousand, even thousands of angels: the Lord is among them, as in Sinai, in the holy place (Psalm 68:17 KJV).

Be encouraged, beloved! Angel allies help bring deliverance!

CHAPTER 6

PEACE AND COMFORT ANGELS

M any times in our lives we need the peace of God that surpasses all understanding—literally. There are holy portals we can tap into to receive the peace Heaven has to offer. Angels bring peace. On many occasions, I've witnessed the peace of God fill my home and my heart during trying times.

> *And the angel said unto them, Fear not: for, behold, I bring you good tidings of great joy, which shall be to all people* (Luke 2:10 KJV).
>
> *And the peace of God, which transcends all understanding, will guard your hearts and your minds in Christ Jesus* (Philippians 4:7 NIV).

Allow the following testimonies shared by those near and dear to my heart to bless you. We all need the peace of God and His holy angels to comfort us during stressful moments. No matter how anointed you are, how many divine revelations and supernatural experiences you've had, you need God's peace during times of trouble and pain. Again, allow these testimonies to minister to your heart. If God released angels of peace and comfort for these people, He can do the same for you.

PEACE ANGEL TESTIMONY
by Hope Scott

Several years ago I went through some trials. During that time, I would go into prayer and worship God. I was releasing the hurt and pain while in prayer to Him. Once while I was in worship, I saw angels smiling at me. I asked, "Are you smiling at me? Why are you smiling at me?" I could not believe God would give me that type of attention. I started crying and releasing more. I have in my journal that the angels were ministering to me. I read Hebrews 1:13 and wrote that Scripture down. As I continued to release myself to God's will, two angels came to me holding vials; they collected my tears and then they went away. They collected my tears in the bottles and flew away. I said, "God, that was weird." I continued to release.

"Vial." I heard the word "vial" and they took my tears away in a bottle. At the time, I didn't know there was a Scripture about tears in a bottle. Now I know that Psalm 56:8 (NLT) speaks of this: *"You keep track of all my sorrows. You have collected all my tears in your bottle. You have recorded each one in your book."* When I read this verse, oh how it ministered to me. God, You have recorded and tracked all of my tears. If it concerns me, it concerns Him and He sees all of that. I've seen angels writing in books. As someone who has dealt with rejection and hurt, I was comforted knowing that He was concerned and is keeping track of that. I want to share with you that He is keeping track of all of our tears and sorrows. He ministered to me and I give Him praise for that.

There is something else I want to share about when I was in worship. In my imagination, I imagined myself on Jesus's lap and I am worshiping Him and talking with Him—and He pulls me in. This particular night when I was in worship, I saw a huge white wing with feathers. It was so beautiful. If you could imagine, it was like being in a white cover and wrapped up in love. I saw and felt this huge beautiful wing cover me. I asked God, "What is this?" Psalm 91 popped into my spirit, particularly these three verses:

Those who live in the shelter of the Most High will find rest in the shadow of the Almighty. This I declare about the Lord: He alone is my refuge, my place of safety; he is my God, and I trust him. For he will rescue you from every trap and protect you from deadly disease. He will cover you with his feathers. He will shelter you with his wings. His faithful promises are your armor and protection (Psalm 91:1-2,4 NLT).

"Refuge" is the word that stuck out to me; God is our help and strength—our place of safety. He is with us, protecting us as written in Psalm 91:14 (NLT): *"The Lord says, 'I will rescue those who love me. I will protect those who trust in my name.'"* When I read those Scriptures it is a reminder that we are to run to Him. Sometimes we talk to and trust in too many people—He wants us to take refuge in *Him.* To take refuge under *His* wings.

God is saying in this season we are to take refuge in Him. That is why I was so excited about the thirty days of prayer Lenika is hosting. God is concerned about everything we do, and spending an hour or two of intimacy to perfect our personal relationship with Him is priceless. I tell my girls, He is a good Father. Whatever it is you are going through, tell your Daddy. He is a good Father and He can fix everything.

That is what I wanted to leave you with. Take refuge, hide in Him. Things are not getting better in the world, and we need to cultivate our relationship with Him to keep from becoming overwhelmed. I thank God for this opportunity to share. I was so nervous and God was telling me to do this in spite of being nervous. I want to encourage and bless you. Angels are real and they are sent to minister to us.

Many times, we underestimate the power of God's love. As my sister-in-love shared her testimony, tears came to my eyes because I knew firsthand what she was experiencing during that season of her life.

PEACE ANGEL TESTIMONY
by Andrea Hardy

I had a vision years ago. I saw a big, beautiful, bright angel while I was in my kitchen. One wing spread across an entire section of my kitchen. I remember sitting down, and when I took a quick look, the wing began to flap and then it disappeared. "God," I asked, "what does this mean?" As an intercessor, I was tapping into the gift and other things God was trying to mold and shape in my life. I had not begun to interpret those things. The Lord said, "I have sent the angel of peace. The coolness of the angel to bring peace." I began to feel a calmness in my spirit. Then the phone rang and it was my mom calling to tell me that my dad had fallen dead on the floor and passed away from a heart attack. God told me that the angel had been sent to prepare me for what was ahead later that day.

There are several Scriptures that tell how the angel of the Lord appeared to Joseph, Mary, and Samuel. God sent an angel to confirm and reaffirm His will for their lives. That is why when we are in prayer, we have to sit down and listen for His voice when we don't have all the right answers. He will send an interpretation through His word to reaffirm and establish His word. If God had not sent the angel, I would have lost my mind when I heard about my father's death—I would not have known what to do and or where to turn. The angel came into my kitchen that day and stood flat-footed and said, "I have brought you peace." As you get deeper into the things of God, He will send an angel to come and prepare you too.

Lenika wasn't afraid to say it to me, this is the season God is working some things out of me, to reveal things I need to do away with. Things I don't need to talk about or think about. God sent an angel to warn me. In the Bible, there are angels who sent words of judgment and about wars. There were also angels who sent prophetic signs and assisted in miracles.

I was researching last night and read that God sent high-ranking angels out to war. Archangel Michael was sent out with power. God sent Michael and he commissioned the rest of the angels to go. To the woman of God reading this, we are led by emotions; but if you have any discernment and have a prayer life, ask God to give you discernment to decree and declare and contact and commission God's angels. When you contact, you locate the angel and then you give it an assignment. I am giving the intercessors that power to decree and declare. If you need the cherubim or the chief angel Michael, if there is someone who needs to be rescued, your business, or your family, call forth the angels to go. God is calling us to contact and commission, fulfill a duty and an assignment. Angels are on location, but you have to give them an assignment. Angels are also on location to give you instruction for the next season.

I believe God is getting ready to do great things and the enemy is not going to stop. It is up to the believers to do great exploits, including supernatural and mighty acts. Woman of God, I want to encourage you today. When God releases an angel to you, ask God for the interpretation. We don't always know what God is saying, so ask Him for understanding. When the angel appeared to Mary, she didn't fully understand, but she submitted her will to God and delivered Jesus. He is going to bring that word back around, that prophetic voice.

Did I get fearful when I got the call from my mother? No, because God's angel prepared me. God strengthened me when He gave me that angel that said, "I have brought you peace." We have the same power and thoughts as Michael. This is not the time to be religious—this is the time to respond. To be forceful and have power and authority and boldness is the key. I hope I have blessed and encouraged you to decree and declare what is to come in this next season of your life.

ANGELIC ENCOUNTERS

by Ayeesha T. Lewis

My grandmother passed away on October 13, 2015; a few days after, maybe even up to a week after her transition, I was riding in the car with my husband on the way to a business meeting. We were in the process of finalizing Grandmother's home-going ceremony, her funeral, around this same time. I was thinking about her, and in a grieved moment I heard a voice in my spirit. It was as if the voice was in my ear whispering to me, saying, "We have been summoned to comfort you. So many prayers have gone up for you. So many people have been praying for you." And then the voice gave these two names, "Gabriel and Michael." I had heard of the two angels before, but had never studied them and didn't know what they did. After hearing this voice, I was curious. So when my husband and I had arrived at the business, my husband went on and I sat in the lobby area and on my phone I Googled the two angel names I was given. I saw that these were archangels mentioned in the Bible. The website mentioned Gabriel as "The Gatekeeper of Heaven" and a "Messenger Angel," and Michael was mentioned as "The Chief Warrior Angel." I was in awe, astonished, and excited that I had this encounter. I felt loved, comforted, and peaceful all at the same time. Shortly after, maybe a few days later, I was sharing my encounter with my best friend, and she told me that she had been praying for me—for me to grow closer to God spiritually.

My Dream

I had a dream sometime between the end of April or sometime in May 2016. In this dream, I remember a glimpse or a flash of six or seven faces—all male, older looking, and various shades of white, tan, and brown. I don't remember details except the last face. He was dark brown with wooly white hair. When I awakened, I heard the voice of the Lord say, "These are your angels." I remember saying, out loud, "They looked old!" and the Lord's response was as a laugh or chuckle, then He said, "What do you expect, they are ancient of days." I remember lying in the bed for a moment in awe, grateful and thankful for the Lord revealing this to me—my angels.

Continuous Encounters

I had continuous encounters with what I believe to be my guardian angel. I was born again in 1996. I may have had these encounters during that time or before, but it was not until the summer of 1998 when I started paying attention to these "sparks" or "flashes" of light. The first time I recall seeing them was in my apartment in August 1998. Then as time grew on, I would see them in different places I would go, even up to now, twenty years later, I still see them. They just show up in a corner, above me, etc. It was not until recent years that I have come to realize that the flashes are reflecting an angelic presence. As I have opened myself up more to embracing the supernatural, I have begun to understand more, their presence. Angels are with us. I praise God for providing them to show up on our behalf and for assisting, aiding, and helping us. Amen.

Angelic Feathers

Another evidence of angelic presence includes angelic feathers. I started receiving feathers since being connected to an amazing Prayer Call. I started listening to Lenika's Prayer Call in 2015 and began receiving feathers in 2016. Up to this date, I mainly receive white angelic feathers, but have also received a brown feather. The colors of the feathers symbolize different meanings. For example, the time I received the brown angel feather, I had recently argued with my husband and was upset. He had left our home to go run errands and I was very upset, crying and frustrated. I decided to take a nap. About an hour later, I awakened as he returned. As I got out of bed to go to the kitchen, a brown feather was sticking up in the carpet in front of my bed. It was small but large enough for me to see it. Brown feathers represent "home" and "grounded." I was so comforted. I thank God for this symbol of His love and care.

The Lord gives strength to his people; the Lord blesses his people with peace (Psalm 29:11 NIV).

CHAPTER 7

AMAZING ANGELIC ENCOUNTERS

PROPHETIC WORDS

One of my friends, Tara, had an incredible angelic encounter. Before getting into her vision of the angel Uriel, I first want to share some meaningful prophetic words.

The supernatural world is more real than our physical world. The supernatural is a real realm. I believe the Spirit of the Lord is allowing me to be more inquisitive regarding this realm. We have to understand that what we seek and pursue will pursue us. I began to get more inquisitive regarding angels—how they operate, move, assist, and how they help carry out the will of God for our lives. I began to receive more impartations and downloads regarding them. As I have been studying, I've discovered that they were very active in the life of Jesus and I wondered why many believers speak about demons more than angels.

I prophetically believe we are going to witness a widespread deliverance with angels bringing forth fire to bring God's people out of dark places. It is time to take territory and occupy the land. God wants us to be all that He has called us to be. Psalm 103:20 is one of my favorite Scriptures. It reveals how important it is—no matter what we are going through and what we are facing and what things are around you—to confess the open Word of God. Angels respond to and hearken to the Word of God.

Last night, I was in my prayer room. I felt fire. Holy Ghost fire. God is visiting His children. We must embrace the supernatural. Heaven is open. The Church will see God's greatest movement. God's Word declares that He will pour out His spirit on all flesh—His sons and daughters will prophesy (see Joel 2:28; Acts 2:17-18). When you study the Word of God, Heaven will crack open. It is time for us to be more alert. I believe this vision that was given to me a year ago. I saw angels waking up people. Getting people up and out of their slumber because there is work to do. There are things that must be done for the Kingdom of God. There are angels sent on assignment to help and assist you.

God instructed me to allow Tara to share her testimony. Tara and I met while in college and we got closer as our children were born two days apart. We were young mothers trying to figure it all out and we grew a bond of sisterly love. Tara shared this fascinating angelic story with me and I knew I had to share it in this book. Follow along as this testimony unfolds. It is very powerful. Other prayer sisters shared angelic visions too, so I included them to encourage you.

ANGELIC ENCOUNTER
by Tara McCloud

In 2012, my daughter and I had temporarily moved in with my sister. My sister had three children—two girls and a boy. We slept in one of my niece's rooms. I can remember being in the bed with my daughter, in and out of sleep. As I began to drift off to sleep, I felt a presence. I remember thinking to myself, *There's someone else in this room.* I was not afraid, but was aware. I opened my eyes and there was a figure in my presence. The angel was so tall that he went up through the roof, yet I could see the entire angel. The angel looked at me and I looked back at him. As I looked closely, I could make out more of his features. I saw a lot of gold, reds, and yellows. When I say gold, I mean like the metallic gold, and it was so bright. While we looked at each other, I thought, *Okay, there's an angel in this room.* It seemed like much time passed, so I asked, "Who are you?" He said, "Uriel." I said, "Okay." I don't recall asking any other questions. I could sense that he was no-nonsense, straight-to-the-point. If I didn't ask him questions, he didn't have anything to say. I went back to sleep.

At that time I worked at a bank and my coworker was a powerful woman of God. I couldn't wait to get to work to share what happened. "Listen, I have to tell you something that happened to me," I said. After I told her, she said, "Hmmm, I'm not familiar with that name." I began to doubt, *Did I dream this or was Uriel real?* As we continued to go through our day, I called my sisters. My one sister is the "Google queen." I shared the story with her and she went straight to do some research. All of a sudden I get all these text messages at work. In sheer exhilaration, I knew that I did in fact have an interaction with an angel.

Then I wondered, *Why did he come to me?* I am going to be honest—the answer did not come right away but years later. I want to be very transparent as I share this experience in my life. At that time, I was reverencing God, but I did not have a relationship with Him. Also, I was questioning my faith. I was wavering a lot through the years. I was hearing all of these stories about others having encounters. I was seeking, wanting, and desiring to have one of my own. Then He revealed to me that I was reverencing Him but not building a relationship. That encounter allowed me to truly believe in God and the supernatural. The supernatural became natural, as I believe it is for everyone. That was in 2012.

When Lenika was talking recently about the fire of God, I remembered that one of the inscriptions I researched said that Uriel had fire in one hand and a sword in the right hand. He is known as the angel of light and the angel of fire. He is a messenger angel. That was one of the things that stood out. I was wondering why I saw those colors. I believe he was brought to me to bring me out and illuminate my heart. It was the glow from those beautiful colors.

I had another encounter in 2017. It was early in the morning before the prayer call and I was taking a shower. I had been working earlier in the year to clean my heart. I had let go of a toxic relationship and was really forgiving people in my heart. I had been meditating on that while showering. Then I sensed an angel was there, and I sensed it was Uriel because that was the only angel I had seen. The way the angel spoke was telepathic. I heard him speak in the spirit and I would speak back to him. The angel of God came to me and instructed me to move my arms to shake off cords and things attached to me. As I began to move, the cords broke off and I could feel myself becoming lighter. I could feel love and peace. God began to download things into my heart. This time it was archangel Michael who visited me. That was my second encounter. I did not see him, but I felt him. He allowed me to feel him and helped my heart remove those attachments of people who had hurt me or my perception that they had hurt me. I was able to walk in love and freedom. I noticed the difference in my heart immediately. I had immediate peace, an immediate breakthrough.

It comes down to realizing that there is a difference between reverencing God and having a relationship with God. We have relationships with our children, friends, and family. Establishing a relationship with God is having a conversation with Him, having a desire and knowing that God is real, carving out time throughout your day to talk to God and listen for His voice. The conversation should go both ways. It is not just for sending up a request or continually talking, you also have to listen. Listen for answers and instruction that will build your relationship with God. I was always talking to people *about* God but I was not talking *to* God. I learned to get quiet and listen for and hear His response—and that is when the shift happened. Listening for God's voice will shift your life into a deeper level of intimacy with Him.

Angel at Work

This experience happened around the same time. I was working part time as a chemist and one day as I was heading to work at four o'clock, a young woman I met and another person were heading home. She is an African-American woman and he is a Caucasian man, and they were walking beside each other. I said my good-byes and, "You all have a beautiful day," and then walked down the hall. For some reason I turned around and saw them still walking beside each other. They were very close, but between them I saw an angel that was walking along with them as they walked down the hall. I thought, *My God, that is so beautiful.* I loved what I was seeing. I loved what I was experiencing.

Angelic Impartation at Home

My friend, Alethia, and I had set up a "Mommy Free Time." We had children around the same age—her child was four and mine was three. One day each week after preschool, she would take my child home with her so I could go off and do what I wanted to do, and one day I would take her child home with me so she could have time to do errands or whatever.

During my free mommy time, I would go home and pray. I would get before the Lord. One particular time, while I was in my dining room, an angel came and stood behind me. The angel began imparting to me right from Heaven. There was a download that took place and it was beautiful. I remember being in a place of worship; as I began to worship God with my hands lifted up toward Heaven, I felt a being behind me who was imparting to me. I didn't want to disturb what was happening, so I just stood there and continued to receive what God was doing through the angel. I knew through the Spirit of the Lord this was a messenger sent on assignment to download and to make an impartation into my spirit.

This continued for a few minutes—a refreshing was taking place through this beautiful experience and tears were streaming from my eyes. There are different times when you may be worshiping God and you may begin to feel different things. Tears may be flowing and you may not be able to feel or see the presence of an angel. This was something I had never experienced before. I knew beyond any doubt that there was an angel ministering to me and imparting. How awesome is that!?

MY DAUGHTER, JAYLA

As mentioned previously, when Jayla was just a baby, about five months old, there were times when it seemed like she was staring right through me, looking at something else. We knew this child was seeing angels. Of course, she couldn't talk at the time; she was barely saying "mama" and "dada," but we knew she was staring at something. As she got older, she would be with me many times during my prayer time. When I was fasting and listening to worship music, she would talk about her experiences—about seeing angels. We thought she was seeing them when she was younger, and when she was older she confirmed that she was indeed seeing angels.

She said she saw them often. One day she said, "Mommy, the angels don't even have to knock on the door. They walk right through the door."

I said, "Really? Is that what they do?"

She said, "Yes, Mommy. There are good angels and I see them all the time."

Jayla shared with me some of her angel encounters. When I asked Jayla questions, she would share her experiences. Once I asked her what the angels did. She said sometimes they would just stare at her and sometimes they would smile. She said that sometimes the angels would be standing up or sitting down. Most of the time she saw them standing in front of the door, windows, or standing in one of the four corners of the house. One time she told me that she saw the angels clasping their hands together. As time progressed, I often asked her questions about the angels so that I would know she was still seeing in the spirit.

One day when Jayla was going to the sink to get some water, I looked into the kitchen and I was frightened. I was afraid because she pulled a chair up to the kitchen counter to get some water by herself. That typically was not something she was supposed to do. She was three, almost four years old, and I paused not to startled her, afraid that any minute she would fall and hurt herself. When I looked up, there was a beautiful angel standing behind her. While she was standing on the chair, the angel stood right behind her, protecting her.

ANGELIC ENCOUNTER

by Jayla

I was very young but will never forget this particular encounter because of how exposed I felt. I was using the bathroom and all of a sudden an angel walked right though the bathroom door. I was shocked but also mad because the angel never once knocked. I finished my business and went to my mom to tell her an angel just saw me using the bathroom. I said to her, "He didn't even knock or open the door, just walked right in." As I think about all this now, it's very funny to me. I was around four years old when this happened.

ANGEL TESTIMONY
by Melissa Cash Freeman

I had been really sick. I was at a Bible study and they were talking about how in the book of Isaiah the Lord whistled. I got face down and prayed, telling the Lord I wanted to hear His whistle. I wanted to hear Him whistle for me so that I knew He was in the midst of us. The next day I went to my doctor's appointment and he gave me a diagnosis of a few different things. I really wasn't sure how I felt about his findings, so I prayed on my drive home.

I stopped at a convenience store to get a snack and I knew I only had a certain amount of money. I had just enough to get what I wanted. As I was in line getting ready to pay, there was a gentleman in front of me who looked a little rough. He was counting out change for his drink and I heard the Lord say, "Pay for his drink." I remember standing there counting the money I had and what I had to buy thinking, *I won't have enough to do all of this. I'll need to put something back.* While I was thinking about it, the man had already counted out his change and went to walk out the door. Well, as I looked up he had his back to the door pushing the door open. He looked at me and started whistling. The look in his eyes I will never forget. I just stood there frozen for a second as he went out the door. I ran to go after him but he was gone; no one was there.

Another time, one my daughters and I were at the mall, and again I only had so much cash with me. We were going to get something to eat at the food court. A lady stopped us as we were walking and asked if we had any extra money. I think she needed it for gas. I looked at what I had and I started to give her all of it, but I thought, *Gosh, if I give her all of this, we won't have any money to eat.* So, I just gave her some money; as she took it, she had that same look in her eyes as the man at the convenience store, which left me almost frozen. She turned around and thanked me. My youngest daughter, Gracie, was with me and she looked up at me and said, "Mom, is that really all you're going to give her?" I turned to give the woman more, but she was gone, completely vanished. It took a couple times, but I guarantee you now I give it all, lesson learned!

This last angelic experience I'll tell you about is when I was in a big city. I had never been there before. It was late at night and I was meeting a friend. I wasn'tfamiliar with the area and I had to go to the bathroom, so I stopped at a McDonald's. Before I could even get out of my vehicle, a man and woman came over and tapped on the window, asking me for money. I told him to go on inside and I would be inside in a minute. I would buy them something to eat. Then I realized where I was—in a not-safe part of town, but I went in anyway. As I was walking toward the door, I realized I was the only person there who wasn't living on the streets. There were several people with their bags by the entryway and in the walkway. The only two people who were actually inside were the people I told I would meet. If was February, so it was fairly cold.

As I entered the restaurant, the cashier was looking at me like I was crazy. I ordered some food for the couple and then a tall man, at least seven feet, came up behind me and started talking to me. I wasn't scared of him. I had complete, total peace. He seemed to have appeared out of nowhere. I didn't see him come in and he wasn't there when I got there. I just kept looking at his eyes. His eyes mesmerized me. He asked me what I was doing there and I told him my husband and I were there for ministry. That was not true because my husband wasn't even with me, I was by myself. When I said that, he smiled and said, "Oh, that makes sense…now I know why I'm here." I thought what he said was odd, but it didn't really hit me at the time what he meant. I went ahead and bought the couple some food, sat down with them, prayed with them, and gave them some money.

Before I left, I went to use the bathroom but the door was locked and I couldn't get in. So as I'm going to leave, there are several men outside the door with their bags. Like I said before, they all appeared to be homeless and they were all talking about how they were going to get me. I had to walk right through them to walk across the parking lot to my truck. Keep in mind it's late at night, the area was dimly lit, and no one really even knew where I was. I wasn't afraid, though. I had absolutely no fear, it was almost like I wasn't even aware of the situation or how dangerous it was. I had such peace. As I walked outside, I noticed that the men were looking atme directly with a strange expression. As I approached, they all moved away, clearing the way for me to walk. They all just sat there staring at me strangely. I walked right to my pickup and got in not realizing that the very tall man, who I believe was an angel, was walking right with me, protecting me and keeping me safe.

ANGEL TESTIMONY
by Patricia Hillard

My eight-year-old granddaughter, Courtney, saw an angel in her room a few weeks ago. She said, "Granny, I woke up and this big, tall angel was standing next to my bed smiling at me. I thought I was dreaming, so I wiped my eyes and closed them and then opened them again…and the angel was still there smiling." She said, "I wasn't scared." She said the angel had big white wings and was very tall.

Tears began to fall as she told me, because I had never described angels to Courtney. Her description was the same as my mom had told me twenty-two years ago, before she transitioned to the Lord. The Lord had spoken to me some time ago about Courtney's special calling.

Angels are intrigued when we talk about them and the Godhead. During a time after receiving a gem from Heaven, I was in the kitchen sharing with my daughters this experience Courtney had. I also took them to YouTube to allow them to hear some of the other experiences shared by other believers. While discussing these angelic encounters with them, I felt a shift in the room. I felt angels were in the room. I asked Jayla, our seer daughter, what was she seeing and she said, "As soon as you started talking about the gem and showing us the clips from YouTube, the angels came out of the prayer room and started pointing at us. The angels were pointing at our conversations and their faces were lit up." This was so beautiful to me because it shows us as, believers, that angels are truly intrigued and concerned about our conversations concerning things of the spirit.

ANGEL TESTIMONY
by Mary Booth

During our intercessory prayer, the spirit of the Lord was in the building. One of the ministers of my church was led to pray for and minister to me. As the Holy Spirit began to move, she was lying prostrate at the altar, praying and interceding for others. At that point, God showed me an angel covering her entire back, arms, and hands. He spoke and said, "Restoration...I am restoring her." The following day, the minister contacted me and we shared the experience. She said that she was feeling herself being "restored." I then acknowledged that God had also spoken "Restoration" to me. It is an experience that I will never forget.

Also, the same week while staying at Lenika's home, I was in her prayer room sleeping and had asked God to reveal Himself through an angelic encounter. I woke up the next morning and there was a white feather lying beside me in the chair in which I was sleeping. And on the day I was going to leave I found yet another feather. God is an awesome God...and worthy to be praised!

CHAPTER 8

CREATING AN
OPEN HEAVEN

Angels bring with them the presence of God. As they ascend and descend from Heaven, there is a crossing over of dimensions, a crossing over and merging of two worlds. As this takes place, we find ourselves experiencing what Heaven has to offer. Open portals, supernatural miracles, downloads, revelation, and *rhema* (spoken words from God) are released. There is a glorious realm that can engulf us as we hunger and thirst after His presence. The presence of the Lord brings supernatural encounters and miracles. There should be a longing in every believer to be taken deeper into the things of God.

I wholeheartedly believe there is a spiritual rain hitting the land:

> *For I will pour out water to quench your thirst and to irrigate your parched fields. And I will pour out my Spirit on your descendants, and my blessing on your children* (Isaiah 44:3 NLT).

God is raining, and there is a rain taking place over His people. I feel rain in the spirit being poured during this time. Last year one of my best friends was in my prayer room in my home and said, "Lenika, I've been feeling a rain anointing." And when I got around her, I could feel it too, like water drops. The other day, one of my prayer sisters and I were on the phone and as we prayed, I felt water, a beautiful heavenly water being released over her. I felt a gushing burst of water. I literally felt it in the spirit realm and God has been saying that His desire is to rain on His people, rain down blessings, rain down miracles, rain down gifts, rain down supernatural promises, rain down provisions, rain down breakthroughs that you know not of. Things you've been pressing in for, the breakthrough that you know that you have seen in the realms of the spirit, the breakthrough that He has shown you. Maybe you can smell the breakthrough; you're so close you can even smell it near. You know how it is when you are outside and before the rain even starts falling, you can smell it? Can you smell God's rain of blessing?

There is a supernatural rain falling from Heaven, saint; and your heavenly Father desires that you receive. God has released His holy angels to bring in the abundance and harvest. Glory!

THERE IS A RAIN OF...

- Abundance
- Spiritual gifts
- Inheritance
- Prosperity
- Miracles
- Mantles
- Fresh oil
- Fresh revelation
- Supernatural angelic impartation

Recently while in prayer, I felt soooo much being released. His promises are being released. I felt God releasing rain on wombs. I've decided to include this section in the book because I believe it is relevant to this time both naturally and physically. If you have been believing God for a baby, don't stop believing. I felt God releasing rain for someone to conceive a baby and I believe this was for more than one person. If you have been believing God to release healing over your womb or healing over your productive area so that you and your spouse can conceive, I pray that you will receive.

> *Be glad, people of Zion, rejoice in the Lord your God, for he has given you the autumn rains because he is faithful. He sends you abundant showers, both autumn and spring rains, as before* (Joel 2:23 NIV).

> *Forget the former things; do not dwell on the past. See, I am doing a new thing! Now it springs up; do you not perceive it? I am making a way in the wilderness and streams in the wasteland* (Isaiah 43:18-19 NIV).

I believe this rain anointing will also be released so that God's people will be cleansed of areas in their soul. Things like trauma and issues they have been carrying for years. Trauma was launched by satan so that the purposes and will of God would be aborted, halted, or destroyed—but God is bringing about a healing and cleansing. There have been certain areas where God's people have cried out, fasted, touched, agreed, placed upon the altar, yet still they have not received a breakthrough.

The river banks from Heaven are pouring over. Prophetically, I believe that angels of the Lord are bringing beautiful containers with Heaven's water within for God's people. We will know beyond a shadow of a doubt that He cares for us and truly has our best interests at heart.

Whatever you have been believing God for, it is time to *receive!* The angels are ready, willing, and able to assist! They are ready to fight battles on your behalf!

God is shifting much in the heavens as it pertains to the alignment of His will and purpose. We must remain in a place where the heavens are open upon us. In this chapter, you will find scripturally sound information to ensure you are creating an open heaven and an environment conducive to angels responding.

ANGELS RESPOND TO...

- Prayer
- The Word
- Prayer and fasting
- Prayer of agreement
- Praise
- God's glory
- The anointing
- Worship
- Repentance
- Obedience to God

PRAYER AND INTERCESSION RELEASE ANGELS

Prayer releases and activates angels. This is a significant part of the life of the believer, which is why Jesus Christ prayed much during His time here on earth; and as a result, the Father's will was accomplished! A life of prayer makes it easier to accomplish the will of God because it brings your will under subjection to His!

- Prayer keeps us from sinning.
- Prayer invites God in to help us with decisions.
- Prayer births things from the spiritual realm into the natural.
- Prayer guards our hearts, it protects our mind, will, and emotions.

- Prayer brings supernatural protection.

- Prayer sharpens our discernment.

- Prayer purifies our motives.

- Prayer causes us to yield to God's will for our lives.

- Prayer allows us to accomplish the will of God for our lives.

"…The kingdom of heaven suffers violence, and the violent take it by force" (Matthew 11:12). Don't be afraid, take all God has for you.

PRAYER AND SPENDING TIME WITH THE LORD

It is imperative that we find time to be with the Lord! Have you ever heard, "Keep the main thing the main thing"? When we set aside time to spend with the Lord, we develop a purer place of intimacy with Him. It is such a beautiful place to be when our hearts are yielded to the Lord. When we spend time in His presence through prayer, praise, reading His word and worship, He shows up and loves on us. He shows up and cleanses us of things that have plagued us through the years, even dating back to childhood trauma and misfortunes. So many supernatural surgeries are performed during prayer. It is beautiful to fellowship with the Lord, and many times things are exposed, restored, revealed—and healed.

Due to busy schedules and the way things are today—careers, children, part-time jobs, businesses—it is not always easy to find time to spend with Him. I recommend making time for Him early in the morning or late at night. I also suggest that throughout the day sing melodies in your heart; on your way to work, turn off the radio and pray, talk, and worship Him. Find brief yet precious time to spend with Him.

But I tell you from personal experience and what I hear from other Christian brothers and sisters, there is nothing like tarrying in His presence for extended periods of time. I share more about this later in the book, but before the tangible anointing fell on my life where I would feel the anointing on me, I would purpose in my heart to spend at least one hour with God daily. I would spend time praying, crying out to Him, worshiping and praising His name. It was through that, and only through that time, I believe that my life was spiritually changed forever.

You may have to adjust something or some things, but it is so worth it! Oftentimes when I minister to other women, but of course this word is for everyone, I encourage them to start small. In other words, start right where you are. If you are not used to spending hours with the Lord, don't go full blast and try to do it unless God anoints you with a grace to do so.

Start with five minutes a day and then increase to ten minutes and then twenty and so forth and so on. What God is looking for is our best fruit, and He is looking for it to come from a pure place. I feel His presence right now! Glory to God! Sometimes we treat God as if He is not God. Lord, have mercy on me; even as I type this, I feel the conviction of the Lord. For example, we give other people—spouses, children, our friends, family members, business partners, or coworkers—more respect than we do our heavenly Father! We give them our undivided attention. We talk with them and even commune with them sometimes for hours and hours. Okay, we women do! But when it comes to our heavenly Father, we can't give any time to Him. Lord, have mercy!

Wanting to be with Him comes from a relationship we have develop with Him. I really believe many of God's people think the only way they can have communion and fellowship with God is by going to a physical building, and that couldn't be farther from the truth. There needs to be a tapping into before we go.

When Jesus went to the Cross and announced, "It is finished," the veil was torn and it gave us access to go directly before the Lord. It is a smack in God's face when His people feel as if they have to go through a man or woman to find fellowship with Him. He is beckoning us, calling us to come higher. He yearns and desires for us to spend time in His presence; spend personal time with Him. He is worthy and greatly to be praised!

Ways we can spend time with the Lord:

- Prayer
- Read the Holy Scriptures (the Word of God, the Bible)
- Worship
- Praise
- Dance before the Lord
- Travail
- Weep
- Meditate on Scripture
- Lay out before God
- Study the Word

The following are Scriptures where Jesus went to the Father in prayer, as well as, Scriptures where He prayed for a specific thing. Christ is our perfect example. If our precious Savior had to spend time in prayer, so should we. His prayers were effective because He spent time with the Father and He prayed according to His will. These Scriptures will bless you and encourage you to pray:

- Matthew 14:23: *And when he had sent the multitudes away, He went up on the mountain by Himself to pray. Now when the evening came, He was alone there.*

- Matthew 26:36: *Then Jesus came with them to a place called Gethsemane, and said to the disciples, "Sit here while I go and pray over there."*

- Matthew 26:39: *He went a little farther and fell on His face, and prayed, saying, "O My Father, if it is possible, let this cup pass from Me; nevertheless, not as I will, but as You will."*

- Matthew 26:44: *So He left them, went away again, and prayed the third time, saying the same words.*

- Mark 1:35: *Now in the morning, having risen a long while before daylight, He went out and departed to a solitary place; and there He prayed.*

- Mark 6:46: *And when He had sent them away, He departed to the mountain to pray.*

- Mark 14:39: *Again He went away and prayed, and spoke the same words.*

- Luke 5:16: *So He Himself often withdrew into the wilderness and prayed.*

- Luke 6:12: *Now it came to pass in those days that He went out to the mountain to pray, and continued all night in prayer to God.*

- Luke 9:18: *And it happened, as He was alone praying, that His disciples joined Him, and He asked them, saying, "Who do the crowds say that I am?"*

- Luke 9:28: *Now it came to pass, about eight days after these sayings, that He took Peter, John, and James and went up on the mountain to pray.*

- Luke 9:29: *As He prayed, the appearance of His face was altered, and His robe became white and glistening.*

- Luke 11:1: *Now it came to pass, as He was praying in a certain place, when He ceased, that one of His disciples said to Him, "Lord, teach us to pray, as John also taught his disciples."*

- Luke 22:41: *He was withdrawn from them about a stone's throw, and He knelt down and prayed,*

- Luke 22:45: *When He rose up from prayer, and had come to His disciples, He found them sleeping from sorrow.*

Heavenly portals were always open over Jesus because of prayer; and as a result, supernatural power was released.

Jesus took Peter, James, and John up on a high mountain, and there Jesus transfigured in front of them. The word "transfigure" means to transform into something beautiful. His raiment became white as snow. The portals were wide open and they found themselves under an open heaven. Moses and Elijah appeared and started talking with Jesus. Peter who was also caught up in the spirit opened his mouth not realizing what he was speaking; however, it was the truth. Then a glory cloud appeared and out of it came a voice from the Father, stating that He was pleased with His Son, Jesus. This is such a powerful demonstration of Heaven touching earth, where the portals opened up and glory was released.

ANGEL TESTIMONY
by Danita Hayes

There was a time in my life when God was drawing me closer to Him, calling me higher in the things of God. I have always had a relationship with Him, but during this time I was really feeling an extreme closeness to Him. So close that I could feel His presence; and most importantly, I could hear His voice and know that it was Him. During this time in my life, my husband and I were having financial problems. In the past, I was always able to depend on my husband to fix everything, no matter what the situation was. Unfortunately, this time, he wasn't able to.

In this season, God did not allow it. This had to happen because He wanted me to totally depend on Him. He wanted me to seek Him like never before and to trust Him with every fiber of my being. It was a necessary process for where He was taking me. He stripped me of everything. I lost some close relationships with friends and family members. I went from working for a real estate company that provided me with security to having to open my own real estate company alone. It was frightening to have to start over and build something new. During this time in my life, God had me in a season of isolation so I could learn to hear His voice above anyone else's and not be afraid to obey His voice regardless of what others thought.

There were times in the middle of the night when I felt my bed gently shaking. I would wake up and look over at my husband to see if he felt it too, but he would be sound asleep. It never frightened me because I always felt a sweet angelic presence and had an inner knowing that there were angels waking me up to go and pray. This happened almost every night for a while. When it felt it, I would get up and go to my prayer closet and spend the most intimate times with God. I would talk to Him and He would talk to me. During this time of prayer, I literally felt my spirit connecting with the Spirit of God. These were times when God would show me visions, give me ideas and, most importantly, spiritual downloads that helped me to grow in Christ. I was so hungry for time with God; some nights I would pray for hours and wake up in the morning in my prayer closet.

As I began to focus on Him more, doors began to open for me in my business and in ministry. The Word tells us that if we seek first the kingdom of God and His righteousness, all other things will be added to us (Matthew 6:33). God already had a plan for my life and He knew the outcome. It was up to me to make the decision to seek Him for direction and guidance so I could walk the plan out. I am grateful and thankful for what He has done in my life and what He is continuing to do. He still has more for me and I will continue to seek Him daily to make sure I am walking in the will of God.

During the times when the angels would come and wake me up to pray was truly an awesome experience that built my faith like never before. Later when I connected with my prayer sister Lenika Scott, she told me about the visions God showed her of angels waking up people in the middle of the night. I was in awe of God's power and definitely knew it was confirmation of what I had been experiencing. The most amazing thing about this is that God will freely pour out His Spirit on whoever wants to receive; all we have to do is ask. Acts 10:34 says that God shows no favoritism—if He can show Himself mighty for me, He will for you too.

As you find yourself in prayer, begin to call upon the Spirit of God and call out the different names of God, as they are in the Word for a reason.

THE NAMES OF GOD

There's nothing as powerful as the name of our Lord God. The Bible says the name of the Lord is like a strong tower; the righteous can run to it and be saved. His name is the only name whereby anyone and everyone can be saved. I sincerely believe the fact that God placed different names in the Word to depict His significance.

He told us to put Him in remembrance of His Word. Therefore, pray the Word back to Him. For whatever need is present, refer to the name recorded in Scripture that meets that need—that is whom you call upon. In other words, if you need provision, call on Jehovah Jireh! If you need healing, call upon Jehovah Rapha! If you need deliverance, call on Jehovah Nissi. Understand?

As you pray and call upon the God, His holy angels are released on assignment based upon the need that is present at the time.

TEN NAMES OF GOD

1. *Elohim* which means "God"; Genesis 1:1.

2. *Yahweh* means "The Lord." Yahweh is derived from the Hebrew word for "I AM"; Exodus 3:13:14.

3. *Abba* means "Daddy, Father"; Galatians 4:6.

4. *El Elyon* means "God Most High"; Psalm 7:17.

5. *El Roi* means "The God Who Sees"; Genesis 16:13.

6. *El Shaddai* means "God Almighty"; Psalm 91:1.

7. *Jehovah Jireh* means "The Lord Will Provide"; Genesis 22:14.

8. *Jehovah Nissi* means "The Lord Is My Banner"; Exodus 17:15.

9. *Jehovah Rapha* means "Healer, the Lord who heals you"; Exodus 15:26.

10. *Jehovah Shalom* means "The Lord Is Peace"; Judges 6:24.

SEVEN SPIRITS OF GOD

1. Spirit of the Lord

2. Spirit of Wisdom

3. Spirit of Understanding

4. Spirit of Counsel

5. Spirit of Strength

6. Spirit of Knowledge

7. Spirit of the Fear of the Lord

Then a shoot will spring from the stem of Jesse, and a branch from his roots will bear fruit. The Spirit of the Lord will rest on Him, the spirit of wisdom and understanding, the spirit of counsel and strength, the spirit of knowledge and the fear of the Lord. And He will delight in the fear of the Lord, and He will not judge by what His eyes see, nor make a decision by what His ears hear (Isaiah 11:1-3 NASB).

PRAYER AND FASTING RELEASES ANGELS

Prayer and fasting create an open heaven. I've witnessed firsthand the Spirit of God move over my life many times when I was not only praying but also fasting.

There are certain things that will just not happen until we fast *and* pray. There are places we will not be able to go until we fast and pray. There are certain realms, levels, dimensions, and territories that we will not be able to tread until we fast and pray. There are levels of success we will not be able to tap into except we fast and pray. There are certain victories that will not be won except by fasting and prayer. There are certain connections that will not be established except by fasting and prayer. There are certain things from which we will not be delivered except by fasting and prayer. There are certain dreams that will not be fulfilled except by fasting and prayer. There are things that just will not be birthed until we fast and pray.

So He said to them, "This kind can come out by nothing but prayer and fasting" (Mark 9:29).

I can go on and on, but the reason for my repetitiveness is that I want you to *really* understand the importance and significance of fasting in the lives of believers. And until we get to a place in our Christian walk where this area is applied, there will be many things that we want to do, have in us to do, but will never be able to tap into or get there until we fast and pray. I hope I painted a clear picture for you. Saint, what we have to remember is that we wrestle not against flesh and blood but principalities, rulers of darkness in high places (Ephesians 6:12). And for us to effectively wage war against the enemy, prayer coupled with fasting must be applied.

PRAISE RELEASES ANGELS

Praise is a powerful weapon. Praise is one of the most effective weapons in our arsenal. Praise will create an open heaven over your life and open major doors, which is one reason why the enemy doesn't want you to do so. Praise activates and releases angels to come down and battle on your behalf, allowing circumstances that once seemed hard or impossible to be moved. No matter what state you find yourself in, never hold back your praise to God. Praise unlocks destinies. God inhabits the praises of His people (see Psalm 22:3).

GOD OPENED A BARREN WOMAN'S WOMB

The womb of a barren mother was opened because of praise. Years ago my coworker shared with me a story about a woman who couldn't have any children. She and her husband prayed and prayed for God to open her womb, but to no avail. If I remember correctly, the Holy Spirit instructed her to keep praise and worship music on in the home and for five months, they did so and God opened her womb. They created an open heaven that released the blessings of God.

In the Bible, the story of Manoah's wife is beautiful, demonstrating the love and power of the God we serve. An angel of the Lord appeared to Manoah's wife and told her she would have a male child. The angel gave her specific instructions, which were to not drink wine or anything unclean. Manoah prayed and asked God to send the angel to them again, and God allowed the angel to appear again. As Manoah and his wife were offering sacrifices to the Lord, the angel ascended to Heaven (Judges 13:19-21). This is such a beautiful story that I highly encourage you to read Judges chapter 13. Praise and worship open Heaven for us. If you want to touch the heart of God, learn how to praise Him.

PAUL AND SILAS

The story of Paul and Silas is so powerful. God set them, and others, free from prison and the chains that bound them—all through the awesome weapon of praise. Paul and Silas were servants of the Lord who were preaching the gospel of Jesus Christ. Then a multitude of people rose up against them, tore their clothes, and commanded them to be beaten and thrown into prison with shackles on their feet. Bless the name of the Lord, because during the midnight hour, they began to sing praises to God, and immediately there was an earthquake that was felt throughout the land. The grounds shook and the prison doors were opened, and everyone was loosed. Read Acts 16:19-40 in God's Word.

Not only did Paul and Silas receive breakthrough, but other prisoners were also freed—and an entire household received salvation!

This story reminds me that praise is such a powerful force and weapon against the enemy. It is easy to praise God when things are going right. But when you offer God praise during moments of great trial, it gets His attention. That is what I call a sacrificial praise. In other words, I may not want to praise God at the moment, but I will humble myself, stop looking at my current situation, and offer up a praise to my Holy God!

PRAISE OPENS DOORS! THERE IS POWER IN PRAISE!

> *When we cried out to the Lord, He heard our voice and sent the Angel and brought us up out of Egypt; now here we are in Kadesh, a city on the edge of your border* (Numbers 20:16).

I heard this story being shared on TBN by a minister who went to Ohio to preach at a revival. During the night of the service, she felt a darkness over the location where the forces of darkness were trying to prevent ministry from coming forth. She saw in the spirit realm black figures, demons, standing and locking arms with each other to hinder the release of the Holy Spirit. After she received the vision, she began to sing praises to God. After praise went forth, she saw the black figures leaving; and as they left, glorious angels came in and positioned themselves wing to wing and held their positions while the service was delivered to the people. She spoke of a glorious time experienced.

Saint, I encourage you to keep worship music playing in your home. Worship is a magnet for angels. They are attracted to heavenly music. We play music much of the time in our home and one day when I returned home and pulled into the driveway, angels were surrounding my home. *Wow!* Before we left that day, I had turned on some praise and worship music in my prayer room.

WORSHIP RELEASES ANGELS

Your entire existence is about manifesting the will of God on the earth. Worship takes our focus off of self and places our focus on our Holy God. The God who is supreme, majestic, sovereign, almighty, omniscient, omnipotent, and righteous.

True worship releases the promises of God. True worship releases angels to operate freely according to Heaven's order. True worship creates an open heaven that allows you to experience amazing encounters and glorious experiences.

Worship is defined as: to honor or reverence as a divine being or supernatural power; to regard with great or extravagant respect, honor, or devotion. According to Strong's Concordance 1245, worship in Hebrew is *baqash,* pronounced baw-kash', and is a primitive root; to search out (by any method, specifically in worship or prayer); by implication, to strive after: ask, beg, beseech, desire, enquire, get, make inquisition, procure, (make) request, require, seek (for).

Strong's 3766 definition for "bow" in Hebrew is *kara`,* pronounced kaw-rah'; a primitive root; to bend the knee; by implication, to sink, to prostrate: bow (down, self), bring down (low), cast down, couch, fall, feeble, kneeling, sink, smite (stoop) down, subdue.

You were born to worship! You were created to worship!

The angels cry, "HOLY, HOLY, HOLY." They bow and worship Him as holy. As God and His angels are holy, we must also pursue holiness. Holy means pure, to sanctify or set apart. When your heart is pure before God, you will find yourself being able to worship Him with ease.

God responds to worship and everything He responds to, the holy angels also respond to. When you live a life of worship, heavenly portals pop open over you.

God is Spirit, and those who worship Him must worship in spirit and truth (John 4:24).

Therefore, I urge you, brothers and sisters, in view of God's mercy, to offer your bodies as a living sacrifice, holy and pleasing to God—this is your true and proper worship (Romans 12:1 NIV).

REPENTANCE

Repentance is an essential component of our salvation and surrendering, because it allows us to see how fragile we are without God. Only through His help can we live a life free of sin. Repentance brings us to a place of true and pure humility before the Lord. When God instructs or leads a person on a fast, one of the first things He deals with is sin. Why? Because one thing that separates us from God is sin, and when we come before Him, His desire is that there will indeed be a connection. For us to be connected to God, we must be clean. Our hands and our hearts must be purified and clean before Him. No matter how many glory experiences we have encountered with the Lord, or how anointed we are, or how many divine visitations we have had, He is the Holy God and we have to acknowledge Him as such. Therefore, purity comes before any of those things and is so important to the Father. It pleases Him when we are pure before Him.

Therefore, repentance is a continual process. Many times in life we endure different trials and sad experiences that cause us to sin; and though it may be unintentional, it is still sin. For example, someone can lose a loved one unexpectedly and such a loss can cause the person to gravitate toward giving in to fear. Because God's Word is true and He instructs us to walk by faith, if someone makes every decision from a place of fear and has their thoughts coming from a place of fear, that person is living in sin. Sad but true. Therefore, a cleansing needs to take place; not only cleansing but repentance also!

I am reminded of David the psalmist who wrote in Psalm 24:3-5 (NIV):

> Who may ascend the mountain of the Lord? Who may stand in his holy place? The one who has clean hands and a pure heart, who does not trust in an idol or swear by a false god. They will receive blessing from the Lord and vindication from God their Savior.

HOW FASTING AND REPENTANCE WORKS

When you fast, you become open to areas of sin in your life. You become sin conscious and your spirit is so sensitive that it begins to reject the sinful nature—thereby repentance comes forth very easily. Fasting breaks down walls of hardness around your heart that keep you from repenting. You will realize what you did was wrong. Doing things contrary to the will of God leads to the way of destruction; it also harms others, and it is harmful to you. To repent is to reject sin. In other words, you love what God loves and hate what He hates. You turn from the things that are not pleasing to Him and you focus your attention on what pleases the Father. Since fasting opens you up and makes you more sensitive to God's holy nature, you begin to dislike walking in sin.

The dangerous thing about not living a lifestyle of fasting and prayer is that sometimes you may not be aware of the sin to which you have fallen prey. During the beginning stages a person may be aware of their wrongdoing; they don't like how it makes them feel, and they don't want any part of it, even asking for forgiveness. But the "it" just continues to happen and then it becomes comfortable to them and they remain in that state, not realizing they now are in sin.

Has this ever happened to you? I'm sure if everyone were honest, we all would say, "Yes, this has happened at some point in my walk with the Lord." Just don't stay there! That's the danger.

That again is another reason why fasting laced with prayer is so important to our souls. We don't want to find ourselves going down the road to destruction and not even realize it. It is imperative to stay in a place of repentance and confession before the Lord.

Confession is very important as it relates to repentance. As God reveals the sin or iniquity of things that need to be repented from, be quick to do so! Remember, fasting allows our spirit to wake up and our ears to perk up in the spirit realm so we can hear Him a lot easier. When we are fasting, many times God will bring things to our attention, along with those areas in our life where we have not repented and confessed.

OBEDIENCE TO GOD RELEASES ANGELS AND KEEPS HEAVEN OPEN

Obedience releases keys and unlocks doors. I've experienced firsthand how the King of Kings has released supernatural breakthroughs because of obedience. During the time I was writing my first book, I received a strong rebuke from the Father. He said to me, "This is an end-time book that has to be released." It was a very strong and urgent call to action. He said, "The level of wealth I have for you will not be received until you finish the book." I was holding up blessings that were to be released to my family. With tears, sweat, and pain, I completed and birthed my first book, titled *Fasting for Breakthrough—How a 21-Day Fast Can Change Your Life.* Instantly the harvest came in and within a short period of time, my life completed changed.

The heaven which is over your head shall be bronze [giving no rain and blocking all prayers], and the earth which is under you, iron [hard to plow and yielding no produce] (Deuteronomy 28:23 Amplified Bible).

As I pondered the words of this Scripture verse, I couldn't help but think about the body of Christ, the current state of the Church, and the vast breakthrough that is yet to be experienced. Although God has greatly blessed my family, I still couldn't help but bring my heart before the Lord with questions: God, what areas in my life have caused blockages? What areas in my life are causing the heavens to be bronze due to disobedience?

No matter how anointed you are, how much God has used you, how many platforms you have graced, there is always room for improving our personal relationship with Him—and understanding this comes from a place of humility.

I personally believe that if we are going to see the manifestations and promises He has for us, we have to come clean and get real and raw, not only with ourselves but real with God. We are living in such an unprecedented time in the world. Wealth transferences galore. God's people being placed in positions like no other.

The fact of the matter is, God's Word is the Word and the Word will never change. The Word of God is final and we cannot compromise the Word and expect change. If we are going to experience an open heaven over our lives, there is a level of responsibility as it pertains to the Word of God that we must adhere to. I write this not from a place of legalism, but from a place of truth. We can't do any and everything and still expect the blessings of God to flow.

As we look at the verse in Deuteronomy 28:23, it clearly shows the difference between an open heaven and a closed heaven. I sincerely believe that because you are reading this book, your desire is to have an open heaven. Your desire is to experience *all* and not some of God's blessings. I believe you wholeheartedly want to receive everything your heavenly Father has for you and you want to walk in His abundance, not only for you but also for your family.

OBEDIENCE

Now get yourselves ready. I'm sending my Angel ahead of you to guard you in your travels, to lead you to the place that I've prepared. Pay close attention to him. Obey him. Don't go against him. He won't put up with your rebellions because he's acting on my authority. But if you obey him and do everything I tell you, I'll be an enemy to your enemies, I'll fight those who fight you. When my Angel goes ahead of you and leads you to the land of the Amorites, the Hittites, the Perizzites, the Canaanites, the Hivites, and the Jebusites, I'll clear the country of them. So don't worship or serve their gods; don't do anything they do because I'm going to wipe them right off the face of the Earth and smash their sacred phallic pillars to bits (Exodus 23:20-24 The Message).

God told the people to pay close attention, to not go against the Angel He was sending because he wouldn't put up with their rebellion. In this Scripture passage, it states that the angel would have no mercy with rebellion. God gave specific instructions and the angel was going to assure His orders were followed.

TITHES AND OFFERINGS CREATE
A FINANCIAL OPEN HEAVEN

God will release angels to help bring in your harvest. You must be encouraged and understand that God knows where your wealthy place is. He knows the vehicle it will take. The angels are ready to take flight to lead you into your Promised Land. Just as Abraham surrendered and obeyed God and was led by the Lord to his Promised Land and his family was greatly blessed, be encouraged that the Lord knows where everything is you need. There are angels of prosperity that God is releasing in the land

and especially during these last days when there will be a true wealth transference and wealth release.

I've heard testimonies of seers' and prophets' eyes opened to the spirit realm and witnessing angels coming down from Heaven during offering time to record the saints' giving. Giving our financial resources is an expression of our worship. It is an expression of gratitude and reverence for Him being our Source. Examine your heart while you're giving. Heaven is not only recording the amount, but also the intent of the heart.

> *Give, and you will receive. Your gift will return to you in full—pressed down, shaken together to make room for more, running over, and poured into your lap. The amount you give will determine the amount you get back* (Luke 6:38 NLT).

I encourage you to give your tithes before any money is taken from your paycheck. Before you get groceries, pay the mortgage or the rent, pay the light bill, phone bill, gas bill, or anything else, be sure that God gets what is His first. He will greatly bless the 90 percent. The enemy would have us think this doesn't matter, but it really does matter—and it is part of the covenant. When the tithes are released back to God, angels can freely move on your behalf in this area breaking off any attacks the enemy would try to bring.

> *"Bring all the tithes into the storehouse, that there may be food in My house, and try Me now in this," says the Lord of hosts, "If I will not open for you the windows of heaven and pour out for you such blessing that there will not be room enough to receive it"* (Malachi 3:10).

While studying angels, I found this verse so profound: "And I remind you of the angels who did not stay within the limits of authority God gave them but left the place where they belonged. God has kept them securely chained in prisons of darkness, waiting for the great day of judgment" (Jude 1:6 NLT).

Watch yourselves, so that you do not lose what you have worked for. Do not lose your place of authority or get moved *out of position* because you are following the wrong person or thing! Alignment within God's will is very important, especially during this era when the Spirit of God is pouring out His promises upon His children. You don't want to align yourself with the wrong person or group of people and miss what God has for you.

TRUE STORY

I was aligned with a woman who was operating in witchcraft and God severed our relationship; He did it so quickly that I didn't know what was going on. This happened right before God took us to a time of restoration; and after the restoration came, God spoke clearly to me and said He couldn't release the promises until she was removed from my life.

When you speak the Word, things happen in the realm of the supernatural. Things are shifted, aborted, reversed, dismissed, brought into existence all because of the power that is in the words you speak. Be mindful. Be intentional. Be deliberate about what comes out of your mouth—for death and life are truly in the tongue (Proverbs 18:21).

Creating an open heaven requires discipline. Prayer, fasting, spending time with the Lord, walking in obedience, living a lifestyle of repentance, and praise and worship are not always easy on the flesh—but so worth it to receive God's favor blessings in return. Keep in mind all these things work by love. Open your mouth and decree and declare to the heavens and earth, that you are ready to receive all your heavenly Father has for you.

The heavens are telling of the glory of God; and their expanse is declaring the work of His hands (Psalm 19:1 NASB).

PRAYER TO RELEASE ANGELS

Father, I come to you in the name of Jesus. I confess any sin knowingly or unknowingly and ask You to forgive me. I repent in Jesus's name. Wash me and cleanse me according to Psalm 51 where David asked for clean hands and a pure heart. I come into alignment with Your Kingdom plans for my life and my family's life.

I decree and declare that angels will release blessings and break-throughs from Heaven. I command angels to be dispatched and released to go and locate every hidden treasure that has my name attached to it. I come into agreement with your heavenly host to bring missed promises, a manifestation of prophetic words, deliverance, Kingdom strategies, wisdom, knowledge, and revelation that is rightfully due to me. I come in agreement that your holy angels will win battles on my behalf. I dispatch, release, and implore Your warriors from Heaven to break up any hard ground in the spirit that is causing my breakthrough to be hindered.

Lord, I commission the angels to release keys from Heaven that will unlock my destiny, strategies, and unlock doors that have been shut tight in the realm of the spirit. I call upon Your heavenly host to fight on my behalf, defend me, bring in my harvest, and execute judgment against my enemies.

We call upon You, Lord, for fresh encounters. Cause Your angels to touch my eyes and place coals over my mouth that I may carry the Word of the Lord upon my tongue that many will be set free in Christ. I call upon Your angels to strengthen me that I may fulfill my Kingdom assignment. I pray to be sensitive to Your holy warriors that I may receive their assistance. This prayer I ask for me and my family in Jesus's name.

CHAPTER 9

ANGELS, PROPHETS, SEERS, AND THE SUPERNATURAL

As we die daily and crucify our fleshly desires, allowing our spirit to reign supreme, we effortlessly connect with the Spirit of God allowing us to enter into holy realms!

We enter into the realms where:

- The supernatural is natural.

- Angels dwell.

- Revelation falls from Heaven.

- Dreams, visions, and visitations become the norm.

- Mantles are placed.

- Secrets and mysteries are revealed.

- The angels cry, "holy!"

- The anointing is released.

- God-given destinies are released and unlocked.

- Signs, wonders, healing, miracles, and those bound for years are instantly set free!

This realm is a true place where we put our flesh under subjection so that our spirit can rule supreme.

Saint! The supernatural is real and it is the will of God for all to experience this beautiful realm. It does, however, come with conditions—we must keep our hearts pure before God and live a life of obedience.

Therefore, I urge you, brothers and sisters, in view of God's mercy, to offer your bodies as a living sacrifice, holy and pleasing to God—this is your true and proper worship (Romans 12:1 NIV).

May God himself, the God of peace, sanctify you through and through. May your whole spirit, soul and body be kept blameless at the coming of our Lord Jesus Christ (1 Thessalonians 5:23 NIV).

You were taught, with regard to your former way of life, to put off your old self, which is being corrupted by its deceitful desires; to be made new in the attitude of your minds; and to put on the new self, created to be like God in true righteousness and holiness (Ephesians 4:22-24 NIV).

PROPHETIC WORD

Angels will help Heaven unlock destinies, reveal callings, and cause people to walk in their purpose! They will help catapult and accelerate God's plans in the lives of believers! Angels will help unlock things that have been buried due to lack of faith or unbelief. For many of God's children, their faith has come under extreme attack causing them to not believe and trust in Him. But faith will be carried on the wings of the angels and they will touch His people so that faith may be renewed again! As destinies are unlocked, so shall faith be and God's children will rise like never before and be a force to be reckoned with. The time of redemption is at hand and God is going to use His heavenly host mightily during these days. Mind, body, and soul healing will come forth in power and demonstration.

I saw a vision of angels that were looking down with beams of light coming from their eyes, much like the fictional character Superman. They were seeking and searching for who is next. Who is next in line for a visitation of deliverance! Who is next in line for a visitation that strength may be released to accomplish the will of the Father. There is surely a thrusting forth of God's Word and the angels of the Lord are going to work with the ministers of the gospel allowing God-given destinies to become a reality!

THOUSANDS OF ANGELS AT MY HOME

One day I went outside to see if the pool was clean or if it needed attention. Shortly after looking at the pool, I turned around, now facing my home, and I noticed that my daughters were in the basement setting the table for the women's brunch I was hosting the next day. As I gazed upon our home, I thought of the goodness of God, how He had blessed my family, and how I desired all of the women who were coming to my home to experience His blessings. As gratefulness and gratitude filled my heart, so did tears fill my eyes and flow down my face. I prayed a prayer of faith, asking God to release thousands of angels from Heaven to my home.

Now this is the confidence that we have in Him, that if we ask anything according to His will, He hears us (1 John 5:14).

Such an overwhelming spirit of intercession hit me and I started interceding for the women. And as I prayed for them to be set free and healed, I could feel something special starting to shift in and around my home. I got myself together and went back inside and our youngest daughter, Jordan, looked at me with big and bright eyes and with much excitement said, "Mommy! There are a bunch of angels in that room!"

I said, "Baby, I know! I just prayed and asked for thousands of angels to come."

She said, "But Mommy, there are so many and they are crammed in that room. One is right there spreading its wings and its wings are going back and forth."

I called our other seer daughter down to the basement to see if she saw anything. Our home is four levels high, three stories and then the basement. I think she was all the way upstairs, so by the time she came the whole way down to the basement, she immediately said, "What's going on, Mommy? Angels are EVERYWHERE! They are upstairs and all over the house!"

As she was making her way downstairs, she saw all the angels that had been called down from Heaven to perform some serious ministry that would take place that next day. Glory to God!

Your prayers have power. *Ask, seek, knock!*

> *Ask and it will be given to you; seek and you will find; knock, and the door will be opened to you. For everyone who asks receives; the one who seeks finds; and to the one who knocks, the door will be opened* (Matthew 7:7-8 NIV).

There were many testimonies of how God moved in my home during the brunch. Days later, reports were still coming. Breakthrough was indeed in the air. The prophetic vein was wide open and it was as if anyone who wanted to speak "Thus saith the Lord," could. All they had to do was open their mouth. The portals were open and they were ready to receive.

During the brunch, after our speaker went forth, our daughter came home from school and I asked her to come downstairs with us because I wanted nothing missed. I knew by the Spirit of God, there would be a vision or word released from her. Because she sees very accurately in the spirit, I wanted to make sure that anything God wanted to reveal to us was brought to light. She came down the stairs and then walked over to tell us that there was an angel, as tall as any she had ever witnessed in our home, standing in our midst, with colors of orange, white, and gold. She said she heard the word "deliverance."

My pastor who was in attendance that day saw angels holding chains in their hands as they carried them out of the house. Chains that had been broken off the women. Hallelujah! Another woman of God was bowed down on her face worshiping God and she shared with us that the Holy Spirit was circling the room very fast. I felt the fire of God as she opened her mouth and shared. Another one of the ladies felt a fire on her foot and a sweetness in her mouth. She was asking the other ladies, "Do you taste that? Do you feel that?" God moved so mightily!

In my heart of heart, I believe that during our brunch together:

- Generational curses were broken.
- Destinies were unlocked.
- Dreams were birthed.
- Identities were awakened.
- Vision was restored.
- Dormant dreams arose.
- Mass deliverance took place.

God was releasing strength and courage for the things He was calling them to launch! The day before the brunch, I sent a message to each lady encouraging them to be "OPEN to RECEIVE"—and they were open and ready to receive! When believers come together, great things happen. And when God sends His angels and the Holy Spirit—even greater things happen!

How good and pleasant it is when God's people live together in unity! (Psalm 133:1 NIV)

That day, vision was restored! Chains were broken. Things holding them back were revealed. What God was calling them to launch would be realized and they wouldn't walk in fear but were empowered to step out into the deep of God's plans for them.

TESTIMONY

by Chandra Jones Williams

The Women of Substance Brunch was truly orchestrated by God. We all knew the angels were present during our time together. At some point, as Lenika was standing beside me during the brunch, she softly spoke that she saw keys. When she said it, I felt a spirit of joy go through me, although at the time I had no clue what it meant to me. But early the next morning, God woke me up at 3 A.M. and downloaded the following into me to share with you!

Praise the Lord, you his angels, You mighty ones who do his bidding, who obey his word. Praise the Lord, all his heavenly hosts, You his servants who do his will (Psalm 103:20-21 NIV).

Angels are the mighty ones who fulfill the Word of God. They obey His voice according to His Word and they are servants created only to do God's will.

The angels release the keys and it's up to us to activate them. Each of us holds the keys within, to fulfill everything God placed in us. When you get in true alignment with God, He will place the people and the tools you need to get done what you are supposed to do. Belief in God and yourself are key components. Stay with God and remain in true alignment with your own purpose in life. You will know when you're fully flowing in your purpose and the calling that speaks specifically to you. There will be a joy and enjoyment with every ounce of your being that you can give back to others as you diligently serve.

God has already placed in you all that you need to live a purposeful and successful life. This life is a journey, not a destination. It is a process of learning what is in alignment with our truest selves, taking diligent steps toward where we need to be daily and trusting that all will work out the way God wants it to go.

Women of Substance—and every reader of this book—you hold the keys, the keys will only work when you unlock and *move* with what is already inside of you!

ANGELS AND PROPHETS

Prophets are called by God. They often receive supernatural revelation and they speak by divine inspiration. Prophets move swiftly in and out of the spirit realm. Because of this, I personally believe there is also a close uniqueness and interaction with angels.

Allow me to use three of my daughters as examples. Three have prophetic mantles on their lives. They all see in the spirit, but two see more visions than the other. This is something they didn't ask for—they were born with this calling. At an early age, two were encountering angels before it was told to them what their callings were. Make sense? This is why I believe prophets are called by God to move swiftly in and out of the spirit realm; and because of the way they were created, it also makes prophets more prone to see or hear in the spirit.

I also believe people who believe they can have supernatural encounters can experience them on a regular basis if they open themselves up and step out in faith. But I also believe supernatural encounters are a natural part of the ministry call of prophets and seers. In the business arena, we often say, what you are seeking is also seeking you. The same can be said of the supernatural things of God. As you pursue God and the Kingdom, which includes His heavenly host, His heavenly host will be drawn to you.

Angels and prophets work together to perform the will of the Father. The people cried out for help, and the Lord sent a prophet and then an angel was released right afterward. In Joshua 5, an angel appeared. In fact, Scripture states it was God's army commander who is the "chief officer" of the host. My personal interpretation is that this was the archangel Michael assisting them.

> *When Joshua was near the town of Jericho, he looked up and saw a man standing in front of him with sword in hand. Joshua went up to him and demanded, "Are you friend or foe?" "Neither one," he replied. "I am the commander of the Lord's army." At this, Joshua fell with his face to the ground in reverence. "I am at your command," Joshua said. "What do you want your servant to do?" The commander of the Lord's army replied, "Take off your sandals, for the place where you are standing is holy." And Joshua did as he was told. ..."When you hear the priests give one long blast on the rams' horns, have all the people shout as loud as they can. Then the walls of the town will collapse, and the people can charge straight into the town"* (Joshua 5:13-15; 6:5 NLT).

REVELATION WHILE STUDYING JUDGES 6

I noticed how the *angel appeared* when the prophet, out of obedience, released the word. It was a hard word, but God sent an angel right after the prophet opened his mouth.

> *Midian so impoverished the Israelites that they cried out to the Lord for help.*

> *When the Israelites cried out to the Lord because of Midian, he sent them a prophet, who said, "This is what the Lord, the God of Israel, says: I brought you up out of Egypt, out of the land*

of slavery. I rescued you from the hand of the Egyptians. And I delivered you from the hand of all your oppressors; I drove them out before you and gave you their land. I said to you, 'I am the Lord your God; do not worship the gods of the Amorites, in whose land you live.' But you have not listened to me."

The angel of the Lord came and sat down under the oak in Ophrah that belonged to Joash the Abiezrite, where his son Gideon was threshing wheat in a winepress to keep it from the Midianites. When the angel of the Lord appeared to Gideon, he said, "The Lord is with you, mighty warrior."

"Pardon me, my lord," Gideon replied, "but if the Lord is with us, why has all this happened to us? Where are all his wonders that our ancestors told us about when they said, 'Did not the Lord bring us up out of Egypt?' But now the Lord has abandoned us and given us into the hand of Midian."

The Lord turned to him and said, "Go in the strength you have and save Israel out of Midian's hand. Am I not sending you?"

"Pardon me, my lord," Gideon replied, "but how can I save Israel? My clan is the weakest in Manasseh, and I am the least in my family."

The Lord answered, "I will be with you, and you will strike down all the Midianites, leaving none alive."

Gideon replied, "If now I have found favor in your eyes, give me a sign that it is really you talking to me. Please do not go away until I come back and bring my offering and set it before you."

And the Lord said, "I will wait until you return."

Gideon went inside, prepared a young goat, and from an ephah of flour he made bread without yeast. Putting the meat in a basket and its broth in a pot, he brought them out and offered them to him under the oak.

The angel of God said to him, "Take the meat and the unleavened bread, place them on this rock, and pour out the broth." And Gideon did so. Then the angel of the Lord touched the meat and the unleavened bread with the tip of the staff that was in his hand. Fire flared from the rock, consuming the meat and the bread. And the angel of the Lord disappeared. When Gideon realized that it was the angel of the Lord, he exclaimed, "Alas, Sovereign Lord! I have seen the angel of the Lord face to face!" But the Lord said to him, "Peace! Do not be afraid. You are not going to die" (Judges 6:6-23 NIV).

PROPHETS AND SEERS

Prophets and seers frequently operate in the realm of the supernatural. It is a way of life for them. When they speak, things happen, people are unlocked, and requests are granted.

Amos 3:7 tells us, "Surely the Lord God does nothing, unless He reveals His secret to His servants the prophets."

Seers

A seer is someone God has called to visually see and interpret things in the spirit that is happening around them as God wills. Just as a person cannot block a dream or a download, whether it be that of revelation, a word of wisdom, or word of knowledge, a seer cannot block his or her ability to be able to see in the spirit. They cannot turn a button on or off to refrain from seeing.

This is such a beautiful gift and operation that is so needed in the body of Christ, as we need to see where the enemy is hiding. We also need to see the angels at work so we can continue to speak the word of God, allowing them to freely ascend and descend on our behalf, bringing the manifestation of what our heavenly Father has promised us.

I heard one of my daughters calling out to me at 3 o'clock in the morning and she was crying, "Mommy, I don't want to see!" In the middle of the night, she had a vision. I rushed out of my room and ran down the hallway to comfort her, but also to pray for her. As I began to pray, before I could say anything contrary to His will, the Lord told me to tell her she was unique and different. He also told me that she would be seeing more. That experience seemed to crack open something in the spirit realm because right afterward, she started seeing even more and has had more vivid visions.

Called by God and anointed for such a time as this, God told me, "You are going to train her and teach her." Parent, if your children see in the spirit, especially angels, encourage them! Read Scriptures with them and talk about it with them. Many prophets and seers are ashamed and embarrassed, they feel like misfits, they feel strange. So, they need your support and encouragement. Teach them about their gift from the Lord, even if you don't fully understand. Ask God questions and He will give you instructions and wisdom to properly train them.

As you are reading this, some of this may resonate with you; particularly if there is a ministry call to the office of a prophet, you will certainly be able to relate to what I am saying. The Holy Spirit will train you! It is a position that is given to you by God and not by any person.

> *Then the Lord put forth His hand, and touched my mouth. And the Lord said to me, "Behold, I have put My words in your mouth"* (Jeremiah 1:9).

The prophet Zechariah had such experiences with an angel sent on assignment to help unfold prophecy during that time, "Now the angel who talked with me came back and wakened me, as a man who is wakened out of his sleep" (Zechariah 4:1).

The Scripture that believers frequently recite are actual words of an angel spoken to Zechariah: "This is the word of the Lord to Zerubbabel: 'Not by might nor by power, but by My Spirit,' says the Lord of hosts" (Zechariah 4:6).

I encourage you to read the book of Zechariah as this prophet had major interactions with the angelic.

If you are unsure about the call on your life, the following are a few signs that may point you in the right direction when you pray to God to reveal your destiny in Him.

Signs you are a prophet:

- A deep intimacy with God

- Deep fear of the Lord

- Repentance is hugely important

- You will see what others do not see

- You feel or see things that come to pass, which seems to happen a lot

- A great need to receive instruction from God before doing anything, making decisions not from a religious or legalistic standpoint, but you seek God as a way of life

- Prayer is very, very important

- Constant need to stay in direct communication with the Father; it is non-negotiable

- Great sensitivity toward sin

- Great sensitivity toward injustice

- Drawn to the prophetic and other prophets; desire more insight, wisdom, and revelation regarding what is prophetic in nature

- Often encourage others to develop a personal relationship with God; you teach and train them how to hear from God for themselves

- When around other prophets, there is truly an unlocking of greater—be it more visions or the gifts of the spirit coming more to life and in operation

- Appear peculiar, even strange, to most people; often misunderstood

You will appear to others as a peculiar person. They will see you as different. That is not altogether bad, but they may think there is something strange about you. Others will not be able to figure you out. Although mentioned in the Introduction of this book, it is worth saying again: you will have to go through major rejection and isolation. In addition, there may be a sense of abandonment. When God sees you getting "too close" to others to the point where you are depending on them and not Him, there will be a quick severing! Sometimes abrupt situations will occur; but as you look back, you realize it was for your own protection. For example, He may suddenly move you from a place or position if He foresees that it will cause defilement.

You will experience a deeper sensitivity to the spirit world of angels, demons, Heaven, and hell. For example, right before a person dies, God may reveal it to His prophets. God has shown me a few people who were going to transition before it happened. He has also shown me people whom the enemy was trying to take out prematurely so that I could stand in the gap and pray. Often during moments of transition, prophets will receive words of wisdom and words of knowledge concerning a person, with specific details.

Not all prophets are the same. Their mantles are very different. Some have visions on a regular basis, and some dream more than others. To some, there will just be a knowing.

If you are called to the office of a prophet, you must keep your heart right and clean before God. And don't get caught up in your title. You have to know and understand that you may miss the mark at times. Pride can definitely cause you to quickly fall. Remember, even Paul had a thorn in his flesh that kept him humble (2 Corinthians 12:7).

Prophetic activation is very important. If you are a prophet, I encourage you to open your mouth. After all, you are God's mouthpiece. When you speak, things will happen, people are freed and requests are granted.

WORD OF CAUTION

If you are called to function in the office of a prophet, you must keep your prayer life laced with reading the Bible, the Word of God. If your prayers and His Word become out of alignment, you can quickly open the door to a spirit of divination. Stay accountable to other ministry gifts.

Have you ever wondered why many of the prophets whom God cleaned up and is now using for His glory attest that before they were even aware of the prophetic calling over their lives they were drawn to the occult or to psychic people, desiring to have a greater awareness of the supernatural? Be very aware of God's calling on your life—use your gifts to glorify God and Him only.

I feel led to encourage you to get acquainted with a few seasoned prophets who bear good fruit, operate in integrity, and have a pure love and heart for Christ. We can learn much from each other when we are all living within His will for us.

PROPHETIC WORD

While standing in my kitchen, I felt an angel standing next to me on my left side. I felt an anointing I've never felt before. It was as if this angel had what seemed like a "duster" in its hand and was dusting my face with it. In fact, it was dusting my left cheek. Later I felt that same anointing around my neck while I was in the prayer room. "Lord, what is this?" The Lord clearly spoke to me saying that He was dusting the prophetic anointing, renewing it: "You used to prophesy accurate and pure words that pierced the soul. You don't prophesy the way you used to." I believe that He was telling me—you—that there is a renewed release happening right now that will prompt pure, prophetic voices to speak!

If you know God has called you to operate in the office of the prophet or gift of prophesy *and* you know you are true prophetic voice for such a time as this, *be encouraged!* The battles have been many but there is a cleansing hitting the land. And I believe just as I felt that "dusting" the other day, many shall feel it as well. The prophetic over your life will return and be restored with power, so *get ready!* The prophetic is coming back with mighty power and purity. Walk in it!

SUPERNATURAL ENCOUNTERS

Glorious Experiences including Gems, Diamonds, Manna, Wine, Oil, Feathers, Gold Dust

I was invited by my sister-in-love Tonya to a home service. She sent a text message stating that angels delivered manna from Heaven for communion and that a gem had appeared in the service, which she witnessed with her own eyes. The next service was in one hour, so I got dressed and headed there with such expectation! When I arrived, they were worshiping. It was the kind of true and pure worship that is not rushed. I think we worshiped God for almost two hours. The services were led by great vessels of the Kingdom. Their names are not publicly known, but these men and women of God spend hours laying before the Lord and they long to do the will of the Father.

Then the minister came forth and started ministering and flowing in the prophetic. She is a woman of God who had died and gone to Heaven. She said the Lord told her that she was not finished here on earth and that she needed to return to preach the gospel, which she does now. God moved mightily in that service! In fact, I was actually able to witness a diamond that flew from the Shofar as another minister blew it! It was beautiful!

Afterward, I asked if I could look through the book where they had taken pictures of the angels who delivered the manna from Heaven as well as the gems, diamonds, gold dust, feathers, the miracle of water turning into wine, and the other miracles they recorded in this book. There were also pictures of holy oil and honey that had been delivered by angels. She said the first miracle of the water being turned into wine appeared a few years ago. They would open their Bible to a verse God wanted them to turn to and manna would appear on the pages of the Bible. Gold particles or gems would also appear right on the pages of the Bible. And angels would come and write messages in the Hebrew language with the manna. They take Communion daily with this Heaven-sent manna and miraculous wine. They filled bottles with water and they would find later that the water in the bottles had turned into wine—just like Jesus's first miracle at the wedding. They confessed the more they share and give it to others, the more they receive.

The next day, which was the final home service, I decided at the last minute to attend, and I was so grateful I did. Worship lasted for three hours! Yes, three hours! I was able to taste the wine, and it was so delicious! In fact, this was nothing like I've ever experienced. They believe there is an impartation with each heavenly delivery. The manna had a sweet taste to me! During worship, there was one point where I lifted my head, and as I looked in the direction where the man of God was worshiping, I actually saw gold appear out of thin air. Again, these are beautiful people who spend many hours with the Lord.

These experiences come not for us to look to them but to look to God and only Him. When I returned home that night, all I wanted to do was commune with the Lord. All of the glorious supernatural experiences made me want to draw closer to Jesus even more!

MY FIRST GEM

My first gem appeared right after God released me to do a public prayer challenge for one month. During the month of November for an hour each day, I encouraged people to spend one hour with God. The stories of breakthrough and refreshing were amazing. On December 11, I went downstairs and there was a gem on my kitchen table. The cleaning lady was in my home cleaning that day and I screamed to get her attention, because my first thoughts were, *A heavenly gem!* Excited but in awe, I asked, "Where did this come from?" She pointed near a window in my kitchen and said she had found it laying on the floor.

I was so excited and told my family, then immediately messaged my prayer partners showing them the video and the pictures of the gem. I was on cloud nine for a couple of days, as I had always wanted a gem released from Heaven since I saw them materialize and appear in front of my eyes in 2013; I mentioned these gems previously in this chapter.

A couple of days after basking in His presence with joy and excitement about the gem, I went to the place in my kitchen where the gem had appeared, and when I looked down I saw something sparkling. To my surprise, it was another gem, which was smaller, and the same clear color as the first gem found. I then thought, *Wait a minute? Could this be another heavenly manifestation…or is this a piece of Christmas decoration from the craft store?* I instantly became sad and my heart started to fill itself with questions. *Lord, was this You? Did the angels bring gems? What's really going on?* Then I started repenting because I mentioned to my family and my prayer sisters that I received gems from Heaven and I didn't want to deceive anyone.

I quickly changed my sadness to, *Lord, if this was You, please show me.* And boy did He show me. A few days later, I started my day as any other day when I'm scheduled to go before the people, I pray and ask Him what would He like me to minister or teach on. I heard a few words but what I kept hearing was the Holy Spirit telling me to wear black. Throughout my years, when the Holy Spirit is very persistent about my outfits, it has always been for a reason. This time was a little different because He kept repeating these words, "Wear black." So I did.

This morning I felt the spirit of peace all around me and I made my way downstairs into my prayer room. Prayer began, and the prayer group and I started discussing His goodness; and since we were in the month of December, we were also talking about our precious Savior Jesus Christ. While my sister Ayeesha was bringing forth the Word, I looked down and saw a gem right on my lap. I got my husband's attention, pointing at the gem. Lo and behold, this gem was the same exact size and color as the first gem that our cleaning lady found in my home and placed on the table. My questions as to whether or not the first set of heavenly gems were of a supernatural nature or not, instantly disappeared. That day I couldn't stop thanking the Lord for His goodness and grace.

Shortly after the gems appeared, when I placed them in my hand, I could feel a heavenly impartation. To God be the glory! God clearly and quickly showed me that He was releasing these precious stones as a manifestation that His holy angels were nearby.

A few months later, we were in our old office cleaning up to transition to a bigger place of business. Also around that time, I was being led by the Spirit of God to take a holistic path toward healing. I mentioned the entire story in Chapter 4, "Angels and Healing." While we were cleaning the final bits and pieces of the office area before the professional cleaners arrived, I saw more gems. I was on the phone talking to my best friend Karen, and screamed out, "Karen, I just received more gems!" They were the smaller gems as before. Karen had just released a prophetic word regarding Gregg and I, and I believe these gems supernaturally materialized as a sign that God was pleased with our transition in business and in my health.

I keep all the angel feathers and gems in my prayer room, and the feathers that I received upstairs, I keep them in one of my jewelry boxes. From time to time I pick them up and smile and thank the Lord for His beautiful ways.

TWO GEMS APPEARED

One day our cleaning lady was at the home and she came to us with two beautiful gems in her hand. This is the same woman who spotted the first gem that appeared in our home. While in the bathroom cleaning, she lifted a box on my bathroom counter and out fell two gorgeous, small gemstones the same exact size as some of the other gems I'd received already.

While I was in my prayer room examining the gems, looking at the color and size, the Lord spoke to me and said, "Give them to her!" I said,

"Okay, Lord," and I walked into the kitchen and told her they were hers. Tears flowed down her face and she told me that she had been talking to God about whether or not she was to continue caring for her sister who she had recently adopted. God was giving her a gift from Heaven to let her know He was pleased with her for taking on the responsibility at the young age of twenty-five to commit to raising her sister as her own. What this also showed me was how God views children and the care of children. Children are very near and dear to God's heart.

KEYS RELEASED IN DUBAI

My husband and I went to Dubai for a much-needed vacation. My spirit was so open and it seemed like everywhere we went, I kept feeling keys fall from the spirit realm. Many times when we travel I can tap easier into the spirit realm. I think it has much to do with familiarity, or the lack thereof. When we aren't familiar with something, we treat it differently, we are more open and sensitive. Also, the principalities over the region haven't learned our ways and can't easily block or hinder us from receiving. At any rate, I felt keys falling left and right and I began to pray concerning these keys. The Lord said, "Some are for you, some are for your family, and some are for My people." My thoughts were, *Wow, Lord, that's some responsibility,* but I was so grateful.

He also gave me instructions about releasing these keys. I felt as if He was letting me know some people, those with pure motives and hearts right toward Him, would receive keys just from being in my presence or being connected to me; and others would receive as I, by faith, released them. My friend Ayeesha had a vision of me going back and forth in the spirit realm with keys. My garments were white and I had loads of keys on each arm and they were for the people of God. The following vision is from another dear friend of mine and the vision she had was in alignment with Ayeesha's vision.

PROPHETIC WORD ABOUT KEYS
by Lady Andrea Hardy

My sister, I hear the Lord say that He's getting ready to take you on a deep out-of-body experience (prophetic trance). In this trance, He's going to place you in the location of your favor. But not only that, He's going to allow you to become the vehicle of favor in foreign countries. I see God elevating you higher. In this trance, you're dropping gold keys—symbolic of wealth, abundance, and authority and dominion. The keys look almost like a rusty color, gold but with an antique-quality look. As you are dropping the keys in these places, the Holy Spirit is going to allow you to help cultivate prophetic gifts and reawaken other gifts that you've been equipped with and assigned to use. When you place the affirmation cards in my hand, that wasn't only an assignment for me to hold. But when I sat down, the Holy Spirit said, "Just embrace the transfer"—there's an anointing that's unlocking for foreign countries soon for you, says the Spirit of God.

A GLORY CLOUD

One of my coworkers and I used to stop in the hallway and talk about the goodness of the Lord and share experiences. But when I became a stay-at-home mom, I didn't see her as much. One particular evening, we met and were talking about our different experiences with the Lord and she started waving her hands. I asked, "Darlene, what are you experiencing?" She said, "I see the glory all around you. I see a cloud around you, Lenika, and it is so thick. I see smoke. Whatever you've been doing in your quiet time and in your prayer time, you stay right there. It is all around you." On that day I didn't see it, but when she began to talk, I felt the glory of God.

There is a place you can get in God where other people who are anointed of the Lord will have their eyes opened. They will see things on you that you may not even see yourself.

Although I didn't see it when Darlene saw it around me, I did experience the glory cloud for myself. At the time, I was going through an ordeal that was causing me a lot of emotional pain. I was actually online studying and trying to search for answers about what I was contending with.

Then God began to talk to me and minister to me about forgiveness. Tears began to roll down my face. I was in our bedroom sitting on the floor with the computer. That day I was fasting. As I looked up from the computer, I saw smoke at the top of my ceiling. The glory had shown up in my home, and I really believe God had sent this as a sign saying, "I have called you. I have anointed you. You are going forward. Do not allow anything to stop you or distract you. I have given you this experience just for you at this particular time." God knew that the weight on me was very heavy. It had come to be very painful, but God wanted me to walk in love and show me love through this process.

I saw the glory cloud in my room. It was as if smoke was coming from the ceiling. I know this may sound a bit crazy if you have never heard about it. But I'm telling you, God is my witness, there was a cloud in my room. It was white smoke, and it just kept coming and falling on me from the ceiling. How awesome is that!?

ANGELS AND A WITCH—AN OUT-OF-BODY EXPERIENCE

I was asleep in my prayer room and taken out of my body when two portals popped open in the spirit. On the right there was a witch. On the left I saw many, many angels coming out of the portal and pouring into my prayer room. Then I saw myself while in the spirit realm quoting Scripture and pointing my finger at the witch. I was saying things like, "His name is above all names! At the mention of His name every knee shall bow and every tongue shall confess that Jesus is Lord." When I woke up, I remember having an out-of-body experience and was very baffled about what had transpired. But this is what the Lord impressed upon me—there are more *for* you than *against* you! Though the weapon may be formed, it won't prosper. *"Don't be afraid," the prophet answered. "Those who are with us are more than those who are with them"* (2 Kings 6:16 NIV). Amen! There was only one witch, but there were many, many angels.

THE HOLY SPIRIT EXPERIENCE

When you start living or are living a fasting and praying life, you will experience different manifestations. One of the manifestations I experienced is coming into contact with the Holy Spirit Himself. This was not God. I didn't realize it was the Holy Spirit until later when God revealed it to me. At first I thought it could be an angel, then the Lord revealed to me it was, in fact, the Holy Spirit.

My sisters-in-love, Dawn and Hope, and I were to attend a baby shower for my daughter's godmother, Mesia. We became really close when we began to grow in the Lord together. When she and Tony had their first baby, we drove from Raleigh, North Carolina, to help host the baby shower. We stayed at Gregg's mom's house overnight because the baby shower was the next morning and Mesia and Tony lived about twenty minutes away. Hope and Dawn shared a room for the night, and I slept in another room with my two small children.

After we went to bed that night, something came into the room. I felt it enter the room; it wasn't a weird, creepy feeling, but I knew it was there and it was standing right beside my bed. It was trying to get me to pray and to go to the room where Hope and Dawn were so we could touch and agree in prayer together. During this time I had no idea that the baby was in danger. I thought all was well because the baby shower was scheduled for the next day which was Saturday. All I knew was that I felt a presence in the room and it was pulling me to go pray with Dawn and Hope.

What I did, because I was not aware of some of the promptings of the Holy Spirit and manifestations of the Lord, I got on my knees and I began to pray. I didn't go so that we could pray in agreement, but I did pray. I understand now that the power of agreement is so strong. The Holy Spirit Himself was trying to use me to go and reach other vessels so we could lock arms in the spirit and pray for our friend. At the time, we didn't realize there was a danger. I went ahead and prayed for her, but not with my sisters. I prayed by myself and then went back to bed.

The next morning when we got up, we received a phone call that Mesia was in the hospital, she had gone into labor and the baby was also in danger. Something had happened with her blood. There were toxins in the blood. All I could think was, *Oh, my God. God, You were trying to get me to pray,* because God saw all that was taking place. The baby had to be delivered. He was premature. He was my godson named Javon. Praise God that he is now a healthy, fourteen-year-old doing very, very well. When I looked back and began to question the Lord, I know beyond a shadow of a doubt that it was the Holy Spirit, the third person of the Trinity who was with me that night. It was not an angel, it was the Holy Spirit!

I share this testimony with you, because once you are intimately in tune with the Lord, He will begin to allow a variety of experiences to take place in your life to teach and to train you. Your prayers and your obedience could save someone's life. It could change the direction of someone's life. There is a difference between God the Father, the Lord Jesus Christ Himself, and the Holy Spirit. The more you stay connected and tuned in, God will reveal to you the different forms of God, the Trinity, and their workings.

PROPHETIC BLANKET

God uses all types of experiences to let people know and understand that the supernatural is real. This next experience I had long before some of the others, during the fall of 1999. Shortly after the initial experience with the Holy Spirit, during a period of time I literally felt a holy blanket placed over me. I, to this day, never saw it, but I felt it. It was as if a beautiful white blanket in the spirit was placed over me. What God revealed was that it was a prophetic mantle that covered me. It was strange because I wasn't used to it, but I would feel it in the middle of the night when I would wake up.

I also remember feeling it when I went to a Rod Parsley conference in 1999. Dawn, my sister-in-love, and I went with our pastors and a few church members. We drove about twelve hours to get there and when we arrived at the hotel to rest a bit before the first service, I felt the blanket covering me. I looked around the room thinking that the other women in the room were also feeling the same covering. It was so beautiful and so peaceful. I believe this blessing came as a result of my obedience to the Lord, consecration, and living a fasted lifestyle.

I also remember during this time, reading the book *The Shaping of an Apostle,* written by June Newman Davis, an anointed woman of God. In the book, she shares her many visitations and encounters with the Lord Jesus Christ Himself. When she was saved in her 40s, she was on fire for the Lord to do His work. She spent many days in prayer and fasting. This book helped me identify and understand much of what was going on through me spiritually. She described a prophetic blanket, but she actually saw the blanket and God revealed to her that it was a prophetic mantle. The vision she described in her book was that of a white blanket coming into her room, over her bed, and then placed over her. This book blessed me—it is anointed. There were times when I picked up the book and opened it right to the page that God was speaking a word to me through. The author also wrote about the prophetic mantle and Elijah's anointing. I wonder to this day if the prophetic blanket I felt on me had to do with the resting of Elijah's anointing.

Remember, there will be times when things happen to you in the spirit and all of the answers are not granted. You don't have the wisdom, the knowledge, and understanding of what is happening to you, but you will know and understand that it is for a divine purpose.

MORE GLORIOUS STORIES ABOUT ANGELS

One time our daughter Jordan saw four angels standing beside me! This happened while I was in prayer and Jordan, who was four years old, was with me. I was in the middle of the walkway kneeling before the Lord in prayer, and though I didn't see any angels, I felt the presence of them. During a point in the prayer, Jordan came over and knelt down with me. After I got up and finished praying, I asked Jordan if she saw any angels. She smiled and said, "Yes, Mommy, there were four angels standing around you while you were praying!" Glory be to God!

Jordan is an anointed child of God, and I really believe by the Spirit of the Lord that she has not only seen angels, but God has allowed her on a couple of occasions to see Heaven. There have been several times when she has told me that she has seen Jesus. One time was around the same time we had lost her granddaddy, my husband's father, my father-in-law. I asked her what He was wearing and she said, "White." When she said it, I felt the sweetest presence.

One time she said, "The angels took me to a place and it was very clean there." She even mentioned seeing some very beautiful flowers. I share this with you because sometimes when we have anointed children, we need to listen to what they are saying. She said that the angels would protect her; and one time when she saw a monster, she also saw three angels there. She said how the angels would smile at her. She referred to the angels being "in place" in the house and seeing the angels fly. I know my baby sees angels.

One time when I was in prayer I was kneeling, and Jordan was across from me in the living room. During the prayer, I felt the presence and peace of God. This child came over and knelt down right beside me. After I finished with prayer, we were talking. She was only four years old at the time. I asked her, "Jordan, while mommy was praying, did you see angels?" She said, "Yes, Mommy. When we were praying, there were four angels standing around you."

I share this again because angels are sent on assignment. They are messengers of God. We are not to pray to them; but definitely we pray to God and ask God to release His holy angels to help, to aid, and also to protect and assist us. How awesome is that!?

Do you have babies in your home who are anointed? Do you have children in your home who are anointed? If they are, listen to them. Many times God speaks through them and sends messages. Listen to the children.

HEAVENLY TRIP

by Leigh Ann Barrett

It was October 14, 2016. The time was 6:35 A.M. I was driving to work from Greensboro to Raleigh, North Carolina. Let me back up a few steps. I just moved from Cary, North Carolina, to Greensboro on October 1. I moved because the Lord told me to. I was feeling sad because it was my birthday, and I was driving to work. I didn't know anyone in Greensboro. I was just being obedient and learning to hear and obey the voice of the Lord.

On my way to work, I was worshiping and praising God. I was thanking Him when He took me in the spirit to Heaven and there was a great cloud of witnesses and the heavenly host blowing party blowers. Balloons and string confetti were falling all around me. Everyone was wearing party hats and were singing "Happy Birthday" to me. Then the Lord took me into a garden and showed me a cocoon cracking open and then the butterfly came out and took its first flight. The butterfly was so beautiful, very colorful. Then as the butterfly flew, I heard the Lord say to me, "Happy Birthday, Daughter." All of this took place as I drove to work.

So, of course, the enemy tried to tell me that I didn't see any of that and I was crazy and didn't go anywhere. How could

I, when I was driving down the road. Well, it was confirmed when my spiritual sister and gift, Jennifer, invited me on October 20, 2016, for lunch to celebrate my birthday. We had made arrangements to meet at 1 p.m. at P.F. Chang's. That morning Jennifer called me to tell me we would have to meet a couple of hours later because she was on an assignment for the Lord. So we met at 3 P.M. We ate lunch and then she gave me my present. Jennifer told me as she handed me the bag that she had my present for several weeks, but this morning the Lord told her to take it back and buy something else. Well, Jennifer explained that she bought the gift and then the Lord instructed her to get it engraved. She was going to have my named engraved, but He told her no. The gift she gave me was a musical globe of colorful butterflies and engraved on the front is "New Life." This was confirmation that the visit to my birthday party in Heaven was real!

THE SUPERNATURAL IS REAL!

There is so much more for us to experience! Great things happen when we lay before the Lord with the expectation that He will come and perform miracles! It is my prayer that something in this portion of the book has activated your faith so that you may believe and trust God on a greater level! I shared many personal experiences; but please remember, God does not show favoritism—He loves us all the same (Romans 2:11 NIV). Seek Him with all your heart and great things will happen in your life!

> *But from there you will seek the Lord your God, and you will find Him if you search for Him with all your heart and all your soul* (Deuteronomy 4:29 NASB).

CHAPTER 10

END TIMES AND THE ANGELIC

John the Revelator was shown the end of time. Guess who showed him? Yes, an angel! It makes sense that if he was shown some of the most dramatic visions by an angel that angels would indeed be used in mighty ways and have a great capacity concerning the end-time movement that will happen upon the earth.

As the end approaches, I prophetically believe we will be exposed to more of the tangible glory of God and angelic activity.

According to the book of Revelation, there are a few things I'd like to highlight that involve the ministry of angels and their work during the end times based on Scripture. The words "angel" or "angels" appear in Revelation more than seventy times, which causes me to believe their existence and involvement is key concerning the execution of the plans of our heavenly Father during the end times. Let's look at a few of the Scripture passages in which angels are mentioned:

ANGELS WILL PREACH THE GOSPEL

Then I saw another angel flying in the midst of heaven, having the everlasting gospel to preach to those who dwell on the earth—to every nation, tribe, tongue, and people—saying with a loud voice, "Fear God and give glory to Him, for the hour of His judgment has come; and worship Him who made heaven and earth, the sea and springs of water" (Revelation 14:6-7).

ANGELS WILL EXECUTE JUDGMENT

And I saw the seven angels who stand before God, and seven trumpets were given to them (Revelation 8:2 NIV).

ANGELS WILL PROTECT GODLY PEOPLE FROM JUDGMENT

After this I saw four angels standing at the four corners of the earth, holding back the four winds of the earth to prevent any wind from blowing on the land or on the sea or on any tree (Revelation 7:1 NIV).

I encourage you to read and study the book of Revelation. As mentioned, I believe the body of Christ will witness more and more angelic visions and encounters. I've listed a few more in this chapter that are related to the topic at hand. May the words of these powerful testimonies bless you.

ANGELIC VISION
by LaTroya W. Handy

I thank God that He has given me experience in knowing that His angels are indeed real. Learning about angels is good, but to actually experience them is something very special and cannot be taken away from me. I cherish the moments when

God has pulled the curtains of the spirit realm back allowing me to take a peek. One such time occurred just a few months ago. I was asleep, as I am every time I have spiritual encounters, and I was praying. I'm not sure what I was praying about, but all of a sudden I could hear a familiar voice praying as well. My ears just popped open to another dimension. This person was actually praying against me. As I heard this, my prayers intensified and I began to pray in the Spirit. As I did this, I could see golden fire being released! In an instant a hand reached down from a peeled-open spiritual realm and told me to, "Come on."

This hand took me to a dimension I had not been in before. It was like I was on a tour of some things in the spirit realm that God wanted me to see. I saw many things. As I moved from scene to scene, I was guided by a strong, fit man. He guided me to each place. In my heart I knew he was an angel, although he didn't really look like what I thought angels looked like. He was strong and had a great muscular build. In hindsight, I thank God, because I do indeed appreciate having a strong angel in my corner! I believe this angel is assigned to protect and guide me. I've actually seen him more than once in my dreams. I am not sure, but in my heart I believe God allowed me to see my guardian angel. I am forever grateful for God's angels.

ANGELIC VISION

by Jennifer Champion

While praying the morning of May 11, 2018, I heard the Lord say, "Release arsenal angels on assignment. Release them over your family, friends, prayer partners, anyone and everyone you can think of who are in direct contact with you."

This hit my spirit so hard. I had never heard of arsenal angels before. I looked up arsenal angels to see if I could find any information, but was unable to find anything. Then I looked up the definition of "arsenal" in the dictionary and found three definitions:

ar·se·nal

- collection of weapons and military equipment stored by a country, person, or group

- a place where weapons and military equipment are stored or made

- an array of resources available for a certain purpose

As the Lord instructed me to release these angels, I saw an angelic figure that appeared to be extremely muscular in stature and he had all kinds of war equipment on him. The size of his muscles reminded me of the "Incredible Hulk" from television and movie fame. I asked the Lord if these were like the warring angels and He said that these were totally different angels that go out and physically stop something from happening!

Behind the angel with the war equipment I could see military equipment. I saw a motor vehicle which looked like a Humvee for the desert that was scaling the coastline back and forth. I also saw a military-type warship with an arsenal of a variety of weaponry on it. I then saw another angel dressed in heavy weaponry do a flip out of the Humvee and transform into a figure that was completely covered in metal. I knew by the Spirit there was no stopping this figure, he would complete his assignment given by the Lord. He had his fists out and they were covered in metal. I could see in my spirit that anything he touched turned to a white powder.

I consulted with a trusted prayer friend in the Lord and asked if she had ever heard of these angels. She had not; however, she had just listened to a Katt Kerr podcast who also saw angels battling and looking like warships. She said the angels turned into actual weapons—they were the weapons! Katt mentioned the angels looked like something in a movie; they appeared like Transformers.

In this season, I believe the Lord is calling us higher and desires to give us deeper revelation of the Scriptures and the angelic realm. They are all around us waiting for us to engage them on their assignments. Dig deeper and ask for the scales to be removed from your earthly and spiritual eyes so you can experience both realms together! He desires us to experience more from His Kingdom to be able to sustain it on the earth.

Rapture and Angel Dream

My husband and I were on business travel. We flew into another city, grabbed some brunch, went to our room, and decided to get some rest prior to meeting with our team. During our time of rest, I went into a deep sleep and started dreaming prophetically. I had a few dreams, but one of the dreams I had pertained to the end times.

In this dream, my husband and I were together and there were people all around. In the sky appeared an angel in the clouds. The angel did a turn in the sky and in its hands was a trumpet. The angel blew the trumpet and immediately my husband and I were taken upward very fast. The dream then changed and we saw last names categorized according to those who were making it into Heaven, those whose names were in the book and who were also raptured up to Heaven. The dream shifted again and at this point I saw myself screaming loudly saying, *"I will preach the gospel. I will preach the gospel. I will preach the gospel. I will do more Facebook Lives. I will do this, and I will do pretty much whatever it takes to get the Word out."*

I sincerely believe time is short and with the work we have to do, playtime is over! We have lives to reach for the glory of God. Jesus's message and truth have to get out. I believe His heavenly host is going to assist us with the preaching of this end-time gospel outreach.

Beautiful Angelic Vision

There was beautiful rainbow in the shape of a feather cloud. This was not a rainbow but a cloud that carried the appearance of an angel feather. Instead of a white cloud, it was the colors of a rainbow. Surely a sign in the sky from God. On that same day, I asked my daughter if she saw any angels and she said they were lined up on either side of the street. I instantly had the interpretation that these were hosts instructed to do some serious damage to the kingdom of darkness. I believe they were not only sent to our particular region but many regions on earth to bring forth deliverance to God's people.

During these last days, God is releasing revelation like never before. When I read Robert Henderson's book *Courts of Heaven,* I instantly knew God was releasing yet another layer to the body of Christ. He was releasing this revelation so that His people may walk in another level of freedom; and this freedom would cause them to move freely in the spirit realm, accomplishing the original plans God has for them. I personally believe more and more visions, transportations to Heaven, and more open visions will be experienced during these times as we draw near to the coming of our Lord Jesus—and angelic help will be more prevalent.

CHAPTER 11

ANGELS AND SALVATION

*In the same way, I tell you, there is rejoicing in the presence
of the angels of God over one sinner who repents.*
—LUKE 15:10 NIV

Prophetically, I believe we are in a time like never before where God's holy angels are going to assist much more regarding souls being added to the Kingdom of God. There will be angels leading people to church and angels helping usher people up to the altar during the call to salvation.

TO THE BELIEVERS

Speaking of salvation, is your salvation secure? I address "the believers" first! Before you close the book and say, "Oh, I'm saved. I don't need to read any further." Please stop for a moment and think about your personal salvation. The greatest breakthrough is that of salvation! The Word of God is true when it asks, *"What do you benefit if you gain the whole world and lose your own soul?"* (Mark 8:36 NLT). We can fast and pray until we are blue in the face, but if we don't have salvation and end up in hell, none of it means nothing.

Many believers will pick up a book and skip over the portion of the book that speaks of salvation, but I felt the Lord wanting me to highlight some very important areas and also make a few points regarding salvation. The first point I'd like to make is about the doctrine that states, "Once saved always saved." This doctrine has caused many believers to be lost. Let's review a few passages of Scripture that shed light on this truth. The enemy has deceived many who believe this doctrine, and for that reason, some who feel as though they are saved do not have their names written in the Lamb's Book of Life.

> *Nothing evil will be allowed to enter, nor anyone who practices shameful idolatry and dishonesty—but only those whose names are written in the Lamb's Book of Life* (Revelation 21:27 NLT).

The Bible is clear and true when it says, "Therefore, my beloved, as you have always obeyed, not as in my presence only, but now much more in my absence, work out your own salvation with fear and trembling" (Philippians 2:12). Living a life of fasting and prayer will help you stay saved! Yes, Jesus Christ died for our sins that we may have the gift of eternal life, but why would the Bible cite words and phrases like "backsliding" and "return to Me" if the once-saved-always-saved doctrine was true? In other words, we are once or were once part of, but something caused us not to be.

Why would there be Scriptures that make a reference to names being written in the book or names being blotted out of the book? (See Psalm 69:28 KJV.) No one can make it into Heaven if their name is not in the Book of Life.

That is why repentance is so important; if people sin continuously and there has been no repentance before the Lord, it can be dangerous and they may lose their lives. They could also lose their salvation because they died in their sin. Many churches don't minister or preach on this truth, but this is cited in Scripture, and is true.

I have read and watched many people speak about being taken to hell, by the grace of God, and they tell about the souls in hell of *people* who were backslidden believers. In other words, they died in their sin without repentance. They knew the Lord, they had once confessed the Lord, but sin got into their lives and they ended up in hell.

Specific stories will not be mentioned in this book, but I've seen videos on YouTube and have also read about many in the book by Mary K. Baxter, *A Divine Revelation of Hell,* which reveals the time when she was taken to hell for twenty-one-days, and then Jesus took her to Heaven. This book reveals countless stories about backslidden believers who were in hell. She also writes about many preachers and pastors and ministers who also lost their souls because they died in their sin.

This is SERIOUS! Either your name is in the Book of Life or it is not. There is no in-between! I caution all believers to sincerely cry out to God and ask Him this question, "Is my name written in the Book of Life? If I was to die today, would I spend eternity with You or would I spend eternity in hell lost forever?"

There is no wonder why the enemy uses the doctrine, "Once Saved Always Saved" as a way to lead many to destruction. Though this does not give a person permission to sin, what it does is send a subliminal message that I can sin all I want and still be saved.

Let me paint a picture. According to this untrue doctrine, if I once was saved and then I went out and murdered, cheated, stole, lied, etc., I would still be okay with no grounds for me losing my salvation. The devil is a liar! Again, that is why *repentance is a daily act!*

Let's look at a few relevant Scriptures:

> *The one who is victorious will, like them, be dressed in white. I will never blot out the name of that person from the book of life, but will acknowledge that name before my Father and his angels* (Revelation 3:5 NIV).

And I saw a great white throne and the one sitting on it. The earth and sky fled from his presence, but they found no place to hide. I saw the dead, both great and small, standing before God's throne. And the books were opened, including the Book of Life. And the dead were judged according to what they had done, as recorded in the books. The sea gave up its dead, and death and the grave gave up their dead. And all were judged according to their deeds. Then death and the grave were thrown into the lake of fire. This lake of fire is the second death. And anyone whose name was not found recorded in the Book of Life was thrown into the lake of fire (Revelation 20:11-15 NLT).

But the Lord replied to Moses, "No, I will erase the name of everyone who has sinned against me" (Exodus 32:33 NLT).

If someone dies without forgiveness of their sins, their name vanishes from the Book of Life. God is the Judge, as His scale is very different from ours. There are times when grace is released over and the person may have time to get it right before death, but why gamble with something as precious as a soul?

You have rebuked the nations and destroyed the wicked; you have blotted out their names forever (Psalm 9:5 NLT).

This may be a hard pill to swallow or even a hard question to ask yourself, but the Word of God is true. God is asking you today, "Is your name written in the book?"

Some signs of a backslidden state:

- Indifference to prayer and self-examination
- Trivial or unprofitable talk
- Disregard of standards of holiness
- Shunning the people of God
- Associating with the world

- Thinking lightly of sin

- Neglect of the Bible

- Gross immorality

If you feel convicted by any of these signs, please repent today and be assured of your salvation. The following prayer is a guide; one you may want to pray humbly before your God and Savior.

PRAYER FOR THE BACKSLIDER

My Loving Savior, the Bible says that You will heal my back-slidings. I come to You because You are the Lord my God, abounding in mercy and slow to anger. Father, the Scripture says that if I return to You, I will be restored. Heal my faithlessness, whatever may be the reason for my backsliding. Forgive my sins and restore to me the joy of Your salvation. You are near to all who call upon You in truth. Send Your Spirit of conviction so that I may confess all my shortcomings to You and You alone.

I come in humility, bringing all my weaknesses to You. Lord, You never despise a broken and a contrite heart. The Scripture says in Psalm 9:18, "For the needy shall not always be forgotten; the expectation of the poor shall not perish forever." So Father, accept me once again into Your fold. Father God, help me so that I do not fall to any temptation, nor depart from You at any cost. Your Word clearly states that it is impossible for a sinful person to please You; but the mind controlled by Your Spirit is life and peace. Endow me with Your Holy Spirit so that I will live a victorious life. Help me to be Your living testimony. I promise You all glory, honor, and praise, now and forever. Amen.

TO THE UN-BELIEVERS

Perhaps you decided to pick up this book on angels because it was intriguing. However, you know you are not saved and you have not confessed Jesus as your personal Savior. The Holy Spirit is convicting you and drawing you closer. Deep down you know that God has called you to do great exploits for His Kingdom!

There is nothing more wonderful on earth or in Heaven as when a person comes to the saving knowledge of Jesus Christ! From reading this book, you know that the angels in Heaven rejoice when a soul is saved and won to Christ! That is so beautiful to me! I have heard ministers who have been anointed in the area of visions, and they have actually seen the angels rejoicing during times of salvation.

> *Likewise, I say to you, there is joy in the presence of the angels of God over one sinner who repents* (Luke 15:10).

It pleases your heavenly Father when a person is saved. Why? Because He sent His Son Jesus Christ to die on the Cross for our sins so that we may receive Him. If you want to accept Jesus into your life, the following Scripture passage will help guide you when you are praying and asking Jesus into your heart:

> *If you openly declare that Jesus is Lord and believe in your heart that God raised him from the dead, you will be saved. For it is by believing in your heart that you are made right with God, and it is by openly declaring your faith that you are saved* (Romans 10:9-10 NLT).

I would also like to bring up a point regarding other religions. Many people, including some Christians, believe that God the Father honors all other religions as long as people try to live a good and godly life and try to stay out of trouble. However, as you will see in the following Scripture verses, this is not the way of God the Father. God will not honor any other religion, and He makes it very clear that it is only through His Son Jesus and His sacrificial death on the Cross that offers people eternal salvation, and thus eternal life with Him in Heaven.

Jesus Christ is the Only Way to Eternal Salvation with God the Father!

As stated, there is no other name under Heaven by which people can be saved other than through the name of Jesus Christ! God the Father will not honor any other name, religion, or faith.

Please note the extreme power and authority on the following first four verses. These first four verses specifically tell us, without any other possible interpretation, that Jesus Christ is the only way to receive eternal salvation with God the Father:

> *There is salvation in no one else! God has given no other name under heaven by which we must be saved* (Acts 4:12 NLT).

> *For there is one God and one Mediator who can reconcile God and humanity—the man Christ Jesus. He gave his life to purchase freedom for everyone* (1 Timothy 2:5-6 NLT).

> *There is one body and one Spirit...one Lord, one faith, one baptism, one God and Father of all, who is above all, and through all, and in you all* (Ephesians 4:4-6).

> *Jesus said to him, "I am the way, the truth, and the life. No one comes to the Father except through Me"* (John 14:6).

> *"I [Jesus] am the gate; whoever enters through me will be saved. They will come in and go out, and find pasture. ...I have come that they may have life, and have it to the full"* (John 10:9-10 NIV).

> *Jesus said to her, "I am the resurrection and the life. The one who believes in Me will live, even though they die"* (John 11:25 NIV).

Then Jesus spoke to them again, saying, "I am the light of the world. Whoever follows me will never walk in darkness, but will have the light of life" (John 8:12 NIV).

And Jesus declared, "I am the bread of life. Whoever comes to me will never go hungry, and whoever believes in me will never be thirsty" (John 6:35 NIV).

I [Jesus] am the living bread that came down from heaven. Whoever eats this bread will live forever. This bread is my flesh, which I will give for the life of the world (John 6:51 NIV).

Everyone who believes may have eternal life in him [Jesus]. For God so loved the world that he gave his one and only Son, that whoever believes in him shall not perish but have eternal life (John 3:15-16 NIV).

Whoever believes in the Son has everlasting life, but whoever rejects the Son will not see life, for God's wrath remains on them (John 3:36 NIV).

Therefore I said to you that you will die in your sins; for if you do not believe that I am He, you will die in your sins (John 8:24).

Most assuredly, I say to you, he who hears My word and believes in Him who sent Me has everlasting life, and shall not come into judgment, but has passed from death into life (John 5:24).

And this is the testimony: God has given us eternal life, and this life is in his Son [Jesus]. Whoever has the Son has life; whoever does not have the Son of God does not have life (1 John 5:11-12 NIV).

And we have seen and testify that the Father has sent his Son to be the Savior of the world. If anyone acknowledges that Jesus is the Son of God, God lives in them and they in God (1 John 4:14-15 NIV).

These verses tell us with certainty that Jesus Christ is the only way to God the Father and His dwelling place, Heaven! God the Father could not have made this truth any clearer than by the way He worded all of these Scripture verses!

Words of advice to help you stay on track—to keep your heart right, your feet grounded, and your ear tuned to God's voice:

1. Read the Word of God daily

2. Spend time in prayer daily

3. Fellowship with believers

4. Fast and consecrate yourself on a regular basis

5. Walk in love

Trust me, when you start to get off track, God always warns. It pleases Him when His children do right and obey Him. Develop the practice of each day *choosing whom you will serve.*

But if you refuse to serve the Lord, then choose today whom you will serve. Would you prefer the gods your ancestors served beyond the Euphrates? Or will it be the gods of the Amorites in whose land you now live? But as for me and my family, we will serve the Lord (Joshua 24:15 NLT).

CHAPTER 12

ANGEL SCRIPTURES

With over 300 verses in the Bible that mention angels, I thought it beneficial to include about 100 verses in this book to help further your study on this incredible subject. I encourage you to become familiar with these instances when angels played important roles in the lives of people in the Bible, and they may show up in your life as well.

Genesis 16:10

Then the Angel of the Lord said to her, "I will multiply your descendants exceedingly, so that they shall not be counted for multitude."

Genesis 24:7

The Lord God of heaven, who took me from my father's house and from the land of my family, and who spoke to me and swore to me, saying, "To your descendants I give this land," He will send His angel before you, and you shall take a wife for my son from there.

Genesis 24:40

But he said to me, "The Lord, before whom I walk, will send His angel with you and prosper your way; and you shall take a wife for my son from my family and from my father's house."

Genesis 28:12

Then he dreamed, and behold, a ladder was set up on the earth, and its top reached to heaven; and there the angels of God were ascending and descending on it.

Genesis 31:11

And the Angel of God spoke to me in a dream, saying, "Jacob." And I said, "Here I am."

Exodus 3:2

And the Angel of the Lord appeared to him in a flame of fire from the midst of a bush. So he looked, and behold, the bush was burning with fire, but the bush was not consumed.

Exodus 14:19

And the Angel of God, who went before the camp of Israel, moved and went behind them; and the pillar of cloud went from before them and stood behind them.

Exodus 23:20

Behold, I send an Angel before you to keep you in the way and to bring you into the place which I have prepared.

Judges 6:12

And the Angel of the Lord appeared to him, and said to him, "The Lord is with you, you mighty man of valor!"

Judges 6:21

Then the Angel of the Lord put out the end of the staff that was in His hand, and touched the meat and the unleavened bread; and fire rose out of the rock and consumed the meat and the unleavened bread. And the Angel of the Lord departed out of his sight.

Judges 6:22

Now Gideon perceived that He was the Angel of the Lord. So Gideon said, "Alas, O Lord God! For I have seen the Angel of the Lord face to face."

1 Chronicles 21:30

But David could not go before it to inquire of God, for he was afraid because of the sword of the angel of the Lord.

Psalm 8:5

For You have made him a little lower than the angels, and You have crowned him with glory and honor.

Psalm 34:7

The angel of the Lord encamps all around them who fear Him, and delivers them.

Psalm 35:5

Let them be like chaff before the wind, and let the angel of the Lord chase them.

Psalm 35:6

Let their way be dark and slippery, and let the angel of the Lord pursue them.

Psalm 68:17 (KJV)

The chariots of God are twenty thousand, even thousands of angels: the Lord is among them, as in Sinai, in the holy place.

Psalm 78:49

He cast on them the fierceness of His anger, wrath, and indignation, and trouble, by sending angels of destruction among them.

Psalm 91:11

For he shall give His angels charge over you, to keep thee in all your ways.

Psalm 103:20

Bless the Lord, you His angels, who excel in strength, who do His word, heeding the voice of His word.

Psalm 104:4

Who makes His angels spirits, His ministers a flaming fire.

Psalm 148:2

Praise Him, all His angels; praise Him, all His hosts!

Ecclesiastes 5:6 (KJV)

Suffer not thy mouth to cause thy flesh to sin; neither say thou before the angel, that it was an error: wherefore should God be angry at thy voice, and destroy the work of thine hands?

Isaiah 63:9

In all their affliction He was afflicted, and the Angel of His Presence saved them; in His love and in His pity He redeemed them; and He bore them and carried them all the days of old.

Daniel 3:28

Nebuchadnezzar spoke, saying, "Blessed be the God of Shadrach, Meshach, and Abed-Nego, who sent His Angel and delivered His servants who trusted in Him, and they have frustrated the king's word, and yielded their bodies, that they should not serve nor worship any god except their own God!"

Daniel 6:22

My God sent His angel and shut the lions' mouths, so that they have not hurt me, because I was found innocent before Him; and also, O king, I have done no wrong before you.

Zechariah 1:9

Then I said, "My lord, what are these?" So the angel who talked with me said to me, "I will show you what they are."

Zechariah 1:13

And the Lord answered the angel who talked with me, with good and comforting words.

Zechariah 1:14

So the angel who spoke with me said to me, "Proclaim, saying, 'Thus says the Lord of hosts: "I am zealous for Jerusalem and for Zion with great zeal."""

Zechariah 3:1

Then he showed me Joshua the high priest standing before the Angel of the Lord, and Satan standing at his right hand to oppose him.

Matthew 1:24

Then Joseph, being aroused from sleep, did as the angel of the Lord commanded him and took to him his wife.

Matthew 2:13

Now when they had departed, behold, an angel of the Lord appeared to Joseph in a dream, saying, "Arise, take the young Child and His mother, flee to Egypt, and stay there until I bring you word; for Herod will seek the young Child to destroy Him."

Matthew 4:11

Then the devil left Him, and behold, angels came and ministered to Him.

Matthew 13:41

The Son of Man will send out His angels, and they will gather out of His kingdom all things that offend, and those who practice lawlessness.

Matthew 13:49

So it will be at the end of the age. The angels will come forth, separate the wicked from among the just.

Matthew 16:27

For the Son of Man will come in the glory of His Father with His angels, and then He will reward each according to his works.

Matthew 18:10

Take heed that you do not despise one of these little ones, for I say to you that in heaven their angels always see the face of My Father who is in heaven.

Matthew 24:31

And He will send His angels with a great sound of a trumpet, and they will gather together His elect from the four winds, from one end of heaven to the other.

Matthew 24:36

But of that day and hour no one knows, not even the angels of heaven, but My Father only.

Matthew 25:31

When the Son of Man comes in His glory, and all the holy angels with Him, then He will sit upon the throne of His glory.

Matthew 26:53

Or do you think that I cannot now pray to My Father, and He will provide Me with more than twelve legions of angels?

Matthew 28:5

But the angel answered and said to the women, "Do not be afraid, for I know that you seek Jesus who was crucified."

Mark 8:38

For whoever is ashamed of Me and My words in this adulterous and sinful generation, of him the Son of Man also will be ashamed when He comes in the glory of His Father with the holy angels.

Luke 1:11

Then an angel of the Lord appeared to him, standing on the right side of the altar of incense.

Luke 1:13

But the angel said to him, "Do not be afraid, Zacharias, for your prayer is heard; and your wife Elizabeth will bear you a son, and you shall call his name John."

Luke 1:18

And Zacharias said to the angel, "How shall I know this? For I am an old man, and my wife is well advanced in years."

Luke 1:19

And the angel answered and said to him, "I am Gabriel, who stands in the presence of God, and was sent to speak to you and bring you these glad tidings."

Luke 1:26

Now in the sixth month the angel Gabriel was sent by God to a city of Galilee named Nazareth.

Luke 1:28

And having come in, the angel said to her, "Rejoice, highly favored one, the Lord is with you; blessed are you among women!"

Luke 1:30

Then the angel said to her, "Do not be afraid, Mary: for you have found favor with God."

Luke 1:34

Then said Mary to the angel, "How can this be, since I do not know not a man?"

Luke 1:35

And the angel answered and said to her, "The Holy Spirit will come upon you, and the power of the Highest will overshadow you; therefore, also, that Holy One who is to be born will be called the Son of God."

Luke 2:9

And behold, an angel of the Lord stood before them, and the glory of the Lord shone around them, and they were greatly afraid.

Luke 2:10

Then the angel said to them, "Do not be afraid, for behold, I bring you good tidings of great joy which will be to all people."

Luke 2:13

And suddenly there was with the angel a multitude of the heavenly host praising God....

Luke 2:15

So it was, when the angels had gone away from them into heaven, that the shepherds said to one another, "Let us now go to Bethlehem and see this thing that has come to pass, which the Lord has made known to us."

Luke 2:21

And when eight days were completed for the circumcision of the Child, His name was called Jesus, the name given by the angel before He was conceived in the womb.

Luke 4:10

For it is written, "He shall give His angels charge over you, to keep you"

Luke 9:26

For whoever is ashamed of Me and My words, of him the Son of Man will be ashamed when He comes in His own glory, and in His Father's, and of the holy angels.

Luke 12:8

Also I say to you, whoever confesses Me before men, him the Son of Man also will confess before the angels of God.

Luke 12:9

But he who denies Me before men will be denied before the angels of God.

Luke 15:10

Likewise, I say to you, there is joy in the presence of the angels of God over one sinner who repents.

Luke 24:23

When they did not find His body, they came saying that they had also seen a vision of angels who said He was alive.

John 1:51

And He said to him, "Most assuredly, I say to you, hereafter you shall see heaven open, and the angels of God ascending and descending upon the Son of Man."

John 5:4

For an angel went down at a certain time into the pool and stirred up the water; then whoever stepped in first, after the stirring of the water, was made well of whatever disease he had.

John 20:12

And she saw two angels in white sitting, one at the head and the other at the feet, where the body of Jesus had lain.

Acts 5:19

But at night an angel of the Lord opened the prison doors and brought them out....

Acts 7:30

And when forty years had passed, an Angel of the Lord appeared to him in a flame of fire in a bush, in the wilderness of Mount Sinai.

Acts 12:7

Now behold, an angel of the Lord stood by him, and a light shone in the prison; and he struck Peter on the side and raised him up, saying, "Arise quickly!" And his chains fell off his hands.

Acts 12:8

Then the angel said to him, "Gird yourself and tie on your sandals"; and so he did. And he said to him, "Put on your garment and follow me."

Acts 12:9

So he went out and followed him, and did not know that what was done by the angel was real, but thought he was seeing a vision.

Acts 12:10

When they were past the first and the second guard posts, they came to the iron gate that leads to the city, which opened to them of its own accord; and they went out and went down one street, and immediately the angel departed from him.

Acts 12:11

And when Peter had come to himself, he said, "Now I know for certain that the Lord has sent His angel, and has delivered me from the hand of Herod and from all the expectation of the Jewish people."

Acts 12:15

But they said to her, "You are beside yourself!" Yet she kept insisting that it was so. So they said, "It is his angel."

Acts 12:23

Then immediately an angel of the Lord struck him, because he did not give glory to God. And he was eaten by worms and died.

1 Corinthians 11:10

For this reason the woman ought to have a symbol of authority on her head, because of the angels.

1 Corinthians 13:1

Though I speak with the tongues of men and of angels, but have not love, I have become sounding brass or a clanging cymbal.

2 Corinthians 11:14

And no wonder! For Satan himself transforms himself into an angel of light.

Galatians 1:8

But even if we, or an angel from heaven, preach any other gospel to you than what we have preached to you, let him be accursed.

Galatians 3:19

What purpose then does the law serve? It was added because of transgressions, till the Seed should come to whom the promise was made; and it was appointed through angels by the hand of a mediator.

Galatians 4:14

And my trial which was in my flesh you did not despise or reject, but you received me as an angel of God, even as Christ Jesus.

Colossians 2:18

Let no one cheat you of your reward, taking delight in false humility and worship of angels, intruding into those things which he has not seen, vainly puffed up by his fleshly mind.

1 Timothy 5:21

I charge you before God and the Lord Jesus Christ and the elect angels that you observe these things without prejudice, doing nothing with partiality.

Hebrews 1:4

Having become so much better than the angels, as He has by inheritance obtained a more excellent name than they.

Hebrews 1:5

For to which of the angels did He ever say: "You are My Son, today I have begotten You"? And again: "I will be to Him a Father, and He shall be to Me a Son"?

Hebrews 1:6

But when He again brings the firstborn into the world, He says: "Let all the angels of God worship Him."

Hebrews 1:7

And of the angels He says: "Who makes His angels spirits and His ministers a flame of fire."

Hebrews 1:13

But to which of the angels has He ever said: "Sit at My right hand, till I make Your enemies Your footstool"?

Hebrews 2:2

For if the word spoken through angels proved steadfast, and every transgression and disobedience received a just reward.

Hebrews 2:5

For He has not put the world to come, of which we speak, in subjection to angels.

Hebrews 2:7

You have made him a little lower than the angels; You have crowned him with glory and honor, and set him over the works of Your hands.

Hebrews 2:16

For indeed He does not give aid to angels, but He does give aid to the seed of Abraham.

Hebrews 12:22

But you have come to Mount Zion and to the city of the living God, the heavenly Jerusalem, to an innumerable company of angels,

Hebrews 13:2

Do not forget to entertain strangers, for by so doing some have unwittingly entertained angels.

1 Peter 1:12

To them it was revealed that, not to themselves, but to us they were ministering the things which now have been reported to you through those who have preached the gospel to you by the

Holy Spirit sent from heaven—things which angels desire to look into.

1 Peter 3:22

Who has gone into heaven and is at the right hand of God, angels and authorities and powers having been made subject to Him.

2 Peter 2:11

Whereas angels, who are greater in power and might, do not bring a reviling accusation against them before the Lord.

Jude 1:6

And the angels who did not keep their proper domain, but left their own abode, He has reserved in everlasting chains under darkness for the judgment of the great day.

Revelation 3:5

He who overcomes shall be clothed in white garments, and I will not blot out his name from the Book of Life; but I will confess his name before My Father and before His angels.

Revelation 5:2

Then I saw a strong angel proclaiming with a loud voice, "Who is worthy to open the scroll and to loose its seals?"

Revelation 5:11

Then I looked, and I heard the voice of many angels around the throne, the living creatures, and the elders; and the number of them was ten thousand times ten thousand, and thousands of thousands.

Revelation 7:1

After these things I saw four angels standing at the four corners of the earth, holding the four winds of the earth, that the wind should not blow on the earth, on the sea, or on any tree.

Revelation 8:2

And I saw the seven angels who stand before God, and to them were given seven trumpets.

Revelation 8:4

And the smoke of the incense, with the prayers of the saints, ascended before God from the angel's hand.

Revelation 11:15

Then the seventh angel sounded: And there were loud voices in heaven, saying, "The kingdoms of this world have become the kingdoms of our Lord and of His Christ, and He shall reign forever and ever!"

Revelation 12:7

And war broke out in heaven: Michael and his angels fought with the dragon; and the dragon and his angels fought.

Revelation 14:6

Then I saw another angel flying in the midst of heaven, having the everlasting gospel to preach to those who dwell on the earth—to every nation, tribe, tongue, and people.

Revelation 16:5

And I heard the angel of the waters saying: "You are righteous, O Lord, the One who is and who was and who is to be, because You have judged these things."

Revelation 22:16

"I, Jesus, have sent My angel to testify to you these things in the churches. I am the Root and the Offspring of David, the Bright and Morning Star."

ABOUT THE AUTHOR

Lenika and her husband, Gregg, are marketplace ministers. Operating as a prophetess, intercessor, and prayer warrior, Lenika lives as a true child of the King, setting captives free through the power of God. Her ministry focuses on obedience to the Holy Spirit and being sensitive to the Father's voice. Lenika is very passionate about seeing others led to Jesus. She and her husband have been blessed with six beautiful daughters.

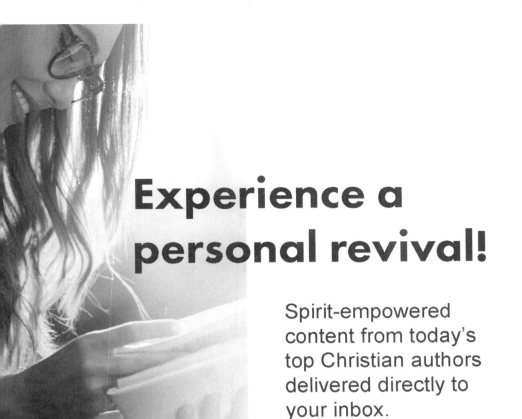